Cause and Effect

Frank Warner Angel's Federal Report on the Lincoln County War

Grady E. McCright

Copyright © 2012 Grady E. McCright

All rights reserved.

ISBN: 1492715182
ISBN-13: 978-1492715184

CAUSE AND EFFECT

Portions of this work were previously published in *Rio Grande History*, Number 12, New Mexico State University 1981 and are hereby printed by permission from University Archivist Austin Hoover by letter dated May 24, 1983.

DEDICATION

This work is dedicated to the memory of my good friend of 45 years and co-author of *Jessie Evans, Lincoln County Badman,* James H. Powell.

CONTENTS

	Acknowledgments	ii
	Preface	3
1	The Department of Justice	7
2	The Killing	14
3	The Pen	20
4	The Inquiry	28
5	The Battle	36
6	The Conclusions	44
7	The Results	56
8	The Later Years	60
	Appendix A,--Lincoln County Report Description	65
	Appendix B,--Charges Against Governor S. B. Axtell	73
	Appendix C,--Charges Against F.C. Godfroy	90
	Appendix D,--Charges Against Dr. B. M. Thomas	99
	Appendix E,--Wallace's Notebook	105
	Chronology	117
	Footnotes	126
	Bibliography	132

Grady E. McCright

ACKNOWLEDGMENTS

I wish to thank all of my many friends who contributed to this work and made it possible.

First, my thanks go to the staff of the National Archives for opening their files and providing much of the original source material contained herein, in particular, Farris Stovel and Donald Mosholder. These two men greatly assisted my friend, Frank Clark, who provided me with my first glimpse of the original copy of the Angel Report at the Archives.

I am also indebted to Austin Hoover, New Mexico State University Archivist; his able assistant, Don Day; as well as the staff at the City College of New York, who provided the only known photograph of Frank Warner Angel as well as much biographical data.

Mr. James Purty and the staff of the New Mexico State Records Center and Archives provided a much needed document on extremely short notice.

Mr. Herman Weisner eagerly dug into his collection and produced documents, and other information that was very valuable to this research.

Last but not least, I wish to thank my wife and family for giving of their time so that this work might be done.

To all the above and to others who had a part in this project go my heart felt thanks. Without help such as this, few works of history could be completed.

The Author

PREFACE

Lincoln County, New Mexico in 1878 encompassed the entire southeast corner of the territory. This vast land mass was nearly 30,000 square miles or about the size of the State of South Carolina; yet by the time the Lincoln County War ignited there were only a couple thousand residents scattered across the expanse. Over 200 of the population were directly involved and participated in the violence, but all were impacted by the conflict.

This land was and is a dry and rugged country and that is the type of settlers who came from a number of countries. They were tough and hardy folks. They had to be to survive. Some of them were down right ornery just like the parched terrain. Many came from Texas and many of those were running from the law or the infamous Texas feuds. They found solace in the territory which boasted of only the sheriff and one to three deputies, if he could keep any at all. The entire New Mexico Territory was patrolled by only one full-time U. S. Marshall. Men rode on both sides of the badge, sometimes deputized for posse work, occasionally authorized, and sometimes rustling cattle or horses to feed themselves. It was a unforgiving land and it contained calloused men who as often as not drew their revolvers first and then, maybe, they would talk.

This huge corner of the region includes in the east the flat, high meadow grasslands of the "Staked Plains" or *Llano Estacado* in the Spanish vernacular. This flat tabletop land that runs all the way north to Canada is named for the wooden stakes driven into the ground when explored by the early Spaniards so they would be able to find their way off the treeless, and seemingly endless tract. This is the area sought after by the large ranchers who were lucky enough to locate a source of water for cattle, sheep, and human consumption, if they were tough enough to hang on to their claims with a gun.

In the western portion of the county, tall mountains push skyward to an altitude approaching 12,000 feet. In the high meadows and canyons along the conifer-forested crags came the smaller ranchers. Along these same streams and water courses, settled the farmers. This competition bred conflict.

The post Civil War period and the reservation bound Indians only increased the traffic seeking a better life on the free land in the west and villages sprung up and the older Mexican settlements grew as the gringos infiltrated the once peaceful area.

Greed and a zest for survival sparked the war and it was more an economic conflict rather than a true range war. The post War-Between-the-States era was a desperate and austere time. The economy was poor, wages were low, jobs hard to find, and those conditions breed unrest. Men stole, robbed, rustled, plundered, threatened, fought, drifted, drank, and killed. As 1878 neared, there were merchants who created economic monopolies and held the poor citizens hostage. In that mix came some decent folks who wanted to break the hold that the powers-to-be held on the citizens.

These do-gooders were not well received by the earlier arrivals who controlled government contracts and could charge whatever they wished because they were the only option in the county. This mix was a prescription for disaster, and on February 18, 1878, it burst into flame.

The Lincoln County War had been brewing for several years but it broke into an open and wind-driven conflagration with the killing of John Henry Tunstall, a young newcomer, rancher, and merchant. Although the conflict had been escalating for several years prior to the shooting of Tunstall, the match that caused the conflagration occurred with his death.

Even after the war slowed, a year later, the remnants lingered on for several years. Many people died and many more were ruined

The Lincoln County War is, perhaps, the best known of the various local wars that occurred during the westward expansion and out of it grew several of our famous or infamous characters of the west. Included in this list is Billy-the-Kid, Pat Garrett, John Chisum, Lew Wallace, Clay Allison, John Tunstall, Alexander McSween, and others.

When the war became so escalated that it was a danger to all the residents of Lincoln County and after John Tunstall was killed, cries went forth in the form of letters, telegrams, and newspaper articles calling for assistance from the federal government. When the intensity of the pleas became unbearable or maybe when the President Rutherford B. Hayes joined the solicited, Washington acted by commissioning a 33-year old Attorney from New York City by the name of Frank Warner Angel to travel some 2,000 miles and conduct and an investigation into the matter. Angel arrived in the Territory in late May to began his formidable assignment.

Angel was educated at the City College of New York and owned a private practice in the city. As he rode into the turmoil, he carried a charter from both the Department of Justice and the Department of the Interior. He was to probe the death of Tunstall, a British subject, who owned a ranch and a mercantile in Lincoln County. Angle was to examine charges of corruption by United States officials in both Lincoln County and similar troubles in Colfax County in the far northern part of the territory. During his assessment, he also uncovered corruption in the Bureau of Indian Affairs on the Mescalero Apache reservation.

Grady E. McCright

    This volume is a report on Frank Warner Angel's findings and his report to both departments in Washington as to the cause and effect of the Lincoln County War and the Colfax troubles. This work will testify to the hard work, insight, and dedication of the young attorney. The shear volume of his testimony is amazing and its completeness is incredible.

1 THE DEPARTMENT OF JUSTICE

IN THE MATTER OF THE LINCOLN COUNTY TROUBLES TO THE HONORABLE CHARLES DEVENS, ATTORNEY GENERAL.

The history of Lincoln County has been one of blood shed from the day of its organization.

These troubles have existed for years with occasional out-breaks, each one being more severe than the other.

L. G. Murphy & Co. had the monopoly of all business in the County; controlled government contracts, and used their power to oppress and grind out all they could from the farmers, and force those who were opposed to them to leave the County.

This has resulted in the formation of two parties, one led by Murphy & Co., and the other by McSween (now dead). Both have done many things contrary to the law, both violated the law. McSween, I firmly believe, acted conscientiously -- Murphy & Co. for private gain and revenge.

Bands of desperate characters who are ever found on the frontier, particularly along the Texas border, who have no interest in Lincoln County, men who live by plunder, and who only flourish where they can evade the law, have naturally gravitated to one or the other of these parties, and are now in their pay, being hired for so much a day to fight their battles.

Gov. Axtell appoints Peppin a leader of the Murphy & Co. faction, as Sheriff, he comes to Lincoln accompanied by John Kinney and his notorious band of out-laws and murderers as a body guard to assist him in upholding law and order (?) McSween then collects around himself an equally distinguished body. The County becomes the elysium [sic] for out-laws and murderers.

A battle is fought--for five days it rages-- more desperate action than was seen on these unfortunate days, by both sides, is rarely witnessed. Both parties desire revenge, and they are now reorganizing, and collecting more desperate characters, (if it were possible) than they previously had. Before I left Santa Fe, it was reported that there were two hundred armed men in the field.

Men are shot down, "on sight" because they belong to one or the other party, and the residents of the County have been forced to take one side or the other either from inclination or necessity. One day Murphy & Co., and his party of out-laws control the County - the next day McSween and his "out-fit" would be the masters.

When these men were not engaged in battle, and when the County seemingly was at peace, they were employed to steal cattle, either from the farmers or the Indians -- a ready market and no questions asked, was found in the persons who held government contracts. If the people protested, they were persecuted and driven out the County.

This state of affairs would be carried to such an extent that it would end in a fight and a war similar to the one now being waged in that county.

During these years the law abiding citizens, or those who would be if they could, have been reduced to poverty by professional thieves, who have made the County their camping ground without the least fear of molestation.

The laws cannot be enforced, for the reason that if the Murphy party are in power, then the law is all Murphy--and if the McSween party are in power then the law is all McSween.

The leaders of these parties have created a storm that they cannot control, and it has reached such proportions that the whole Territory cannot put it down. Lands go uncultivated; ranches are abandoned; merchants have closed their stores; citizens have left the homes they have occupied for years; business has ceased, and lawlessness and murder are the order of the day.

These outlaws who prowl the County with the avowed purpose of murder, who have no interest in the County or wrongs of their own to redress, no matter on which side they belong, should be hunted **down**, and made to answer for their crimes.

The Territory has no militia, and the County being in the hands of these armed outlaws, the laws and mandates of the courts cannot be enforced or respected, nor lives or property protected. It is impossible for even the Courts to be held.

I would respectfully refer to my report to the Interior Department on the charges against Governor Axtell as to the additional causes for the existing troubles in Lincoln County.

I would most respectfully recommend that such assistance be given to the governor of New Mexico that the laws may be enforced and respected, and life and property protected. All of which is respectfully submitted.

Washington, October 7th 1878.

{signed) Frank Warner Angel

Special Agent

Thus reads the summation of one of the American West's most complete records of frontier lawlessness, the official report of Special Agent Frank Warner Angel, analyzing the troubled conditions that existed in New Mexico Territory in 1878. Many had already died and more were to follow. This was the West as popular fiction has immortalized it. Men were killed on the streets for little cause, but this was the frontier and men settled their differences, by and large, without the assistance of bona fide lawmen or courts. Each protected his life and property as he felt necessary, more often than not with a gun.

When the difficulties became unbearable and the citizens appealed to higher authority for assistance. Angel was commissioned by the federal government to determine the causes and responsible parties involved in the February 1878 murder of John Henry Tunstall, a British subject. Angel did a thorough job and he interviewed a large portion of the population of the sparsely settled County. Upon his return from the territory, he filed a report with voluminous supporting evidence. This document is possibly the most detailed primary source available on the famous civilian conflict.

This account of the Angel report on Lincoln County is intended to acquaint the reader with Frank Angel, his investigation of Tunstall's death, his conclusions, and the evidence he gathered in support of them. Although some of Angels views are supported by historians, others are not. This narrative summarizes Angel's findings, including those that are in conflict with previously published opinions.

Lincoln County encompassed an immense tract of land in the southeast corner of the territory larger than the present State of Ohio; yet within its borders lived only about 2,000 residents. The turbulence had touched almost everyone.

Trouble had been brewing for most of the years since the Apaches had been confined to the reservation and immigrants began to relocate to the arid and rugged country that was so wide open and ripe for settlers. The Mexican population had been in the area for generations but when the white men arrived and started creating a monopoly on the business interests in the area, unrest surfaced. In the late 1870's additional *gringos* moved into the area and decided to test the awarding of government contracts and the merchant's hold on the residents, unrest escalated into disorder.

One of the interlopers was John H. Tunstall, a well-bread Englishman from a wealthy family in London. Tunstall left England to seek his fortune with a healthy stipend from his father. After some traveling about the world, he arrived in Lincoln County in late 1876 to make his mark in the rather lucrative cattle industry. Before long, he and a lawyer named Alexander McSween, a recent addition to the Territory decided that there was money to be made by opening a mercantile store in the village of Lincoln, the County Seat, and competing with well established L. G. Murphy & Company which held the government contract for nearby Fort Stanton and the Apache Reservation. It proved to be a fatal decision for both gatecrashers.

Frank Warner Angel: Graduation picture taken in June, 1868. (Courtesy The City College of New York)

2 THE KILLING

Dawn broke clear and bright on February 18, 1878 as it does most winter mornings in the Sacramento Mountains of southern New Mexico. Before the sun set, the smoldering bitterness in Lincoln County was fanned into an inferno that engulfed most all its 2,000 residents.

Shortly after first light, on a small ranch nestled peacefully along the Rio Feliz, several men rose from breakfast and ambled out to the corral. They saddled their mounts and assembled a string of eight horses for the drive into Lincoln, the county seat.

The owner of the ranch was John Henry Tunstall from London. Assisting him with the herd were William Bonney, later to be known as "Billy-the-Kid;" Richard (Dick) Brewer, a nearby rancher and part-time foreman of the Tunstall spread; Robert Widenmann, a Deputy United States Marshall; John Middleton, a redoubtable gunfighter; and Fred Waite, a friend of Bonney's and fellow Tunstall employee.

Leaving the ranch shortly after 8 a.m., the men made their way slowly north along the road with Waite driving a wagon. About halfway to Lincoln, a small trail veered off to the west and passed through rough country before crossing the Ruidoso River and continuing into town. Although much shorter than the road, this route was not suited for wagon use, so Waite kept the team on the main road while the rest of the party took the trail.

By late afternoon, the drovers were leisurely drifting along some ten miles from Lincoln. They had allowed the herd to become so strung out along the trail that 500 yards separated Tunstall, Widenmann, and Brewer at the head of the horses from Bonney and Middleton, riding drag.

Suddenly, a flock of turkeys flushed. Brewer and Widenmann, unable to resist the challenge, gave chase. Tunstall remained with the horses but urged the two hunters on by yelling encouragement. Pursuing the birds over a small hill and up the side of the next, Widenmann and Brewer lost sight of the *remuda*.

Bonney and Middleton meanwhile were startled by the sickening whine of a bullet passing overhead and the sharp crack of a rifle. They wheeled and discovered a large group of men bearing down on them from behind. Although there had been no shout of warning, the newcomers were obviously intent on doing the Tunstall part no good. Wise to the ways of the frontier, Bonney and Middleton abandoned the herd, and screaming for Tunstall to follow, headed in the direction Brewer and Widenmann had taken. The turkey hunters sensed what was happening, and dismissed the birds as they sprinted toward a rocky hillside which afforded better protection.

The firing stopped as the raiders spotted Tunstall and ignored the fleeing drovers. The shooters galloped straight through the scattering herd to the Englishman.

Just before reaching their rocky sanctuary, Tunstall's men noted that their leader was still on the trail facing the charge. By the time the foursome dismounted and found protection among the boulders, they could no longer see Tunstall or the leaders of the hostile group because of the terrain.

Two more shots echoed across the canyons. Then, all was

quiet. After what seemed an eternity, John Middleton muttered everyone's fears, "They've killed Tunstall[1]."

    Mounting up, the remaining four continued their trek to Lincoln without returning to the trail. They knew there was nothing they could do to help their boss. It was well after dark when they arrived in Lincoln bringing the first news of the murder.

John Henry Tunstall: His business activities in Lincoln threatened the Murphy/Dolan enterprises. (Courtesy M. G. Fulton Collection, Special Collections, University of Arizona Library.)

Lincoln, New Mexico: The Murphy-Dolan Store can be seen in the left foreground by the water tank. Tunstall's store is on the opposite side of the street about three-fourths down its length. It is the longest building on that side of the street.. (Courtesy M. G. Fulton Collection, Special Collections, University of Arizona Library)

CAUSE AND EFFECT

The Tunstall store in Lincoln: (Courtesy of the
Old Lincoln County Memorial Commission)

3 THE PEN

Tunstall's body lay where it fell until the next morning when, at the request of Tunstall's business partner, Alexander McSween,[2] local rancher John B. Newcomb loaded the body into his wagon and hauled it to Lincoln.[3] Soon after its arrival, a coroner's inquest convened and identified the body, cause of death, and probable killers. The following day, a post-mortem was conducted by Dr. D. M. Appel, Fort Stanton's post surgeon, assisted by Dr. T. F. Ealy, a physician and minister in Lincoln.[4] The body was also embalmed. On Friday, February 22, Tunstall was laid to rest in a plot along the quiet Rio Bonito River just east of his general mercantile store.

Almost before Tunstall's grave was closed, McSween went to work. On the 25th, he wrote a letter to Sir Edward Thornton, the British representative in Washington, D.C. informing him of Tunstall's murder and requesting assistance in bringing about an impartial investigation. Robert Widenmann followed this letter with one of his own the next day.[5]

Armed with these two letters and concerned over the death of a fellow Britisher, Thornton wrote to the United States Secretary of State, William M. Evarts, stating:

My attention has been called to the murder of John H. Tunstall, a British subject, which is stated to have taken place in the county of Lincoln, New Mexico, eleven miles from the town of Lincoln, on the afternoon of 18th ultimo, and to have been committed by one James J. Dolan and others....

It appears that after the murderers arrived in the town of Lincoln, Mr. A. A. McSween obtained warrants for their arrest, and put them in the hands of a constable in order that the criminals might be apprehended. He did not deliver them to the Sheriff of the County because he believed that the officer was indirectly connected with the murder. When the constable and posse went to serve the warrants he was met by the Sheriff who made them prisoners, and refused to allow them to make any arrests, though the alleged murderers of Mr. Tunstall were then and there with the Sheriff.

If the above mentioned statements be true, it would appear that a most inexcusable murder has been committed, and that the Sheriff of the County instead of assisting in the arrest of the murderers, as he is duty bound, is impeding the course of justice. Under these circumstances I cannot doubt that the Government of the United States will promptly cause inquiries to be made into the matter and will take such measures as it may deem expedient for investigating the conduct of the Sheriff of Lincoln County and for ensuring the arrest of the accused and their being brought to trial.[6].

Secretary of State Evarts forwarded the letter to Charles Devens, United States Attorney General saying, "I will thank you to cause proper inquiry to be made into the facts...and advise this department of the results."

S. F. Phillips, the acting Attorney General, forwarded copies of Evarts and Thornton's letters to Thomas B. Catron, United States District Attorney for New Mexico, reiterating, "At the request of the Secretary you will please make prompt inquiry into the circumstances attending this murder and report fully to me with a statement of what measures have been or can be taken to bring to punishment the parties guilty of this crime."

During this same period, Montague R. Leverson,[7] a transient scout and aspiring colonizer, wrote twice to United States Senator H. B. Anthony of Rhode Island, updating the news on the situation in Lincoln County and urging that action be taken. The Senator forwarded the communiqués to Secretary of the Interior Carl Schurz, who, in turn, sent them to the United States Attorney General's office.

Leverson then wrote to none other than Rutherford B. Hayes, President of the United States, requesting that Territorial Governor Samuel B. Axtell be suspended (an appointment Leverson coveted), that United States District Attorney Thomas B. Catron be removed and his records confiscated, and the 3rd Judicial District's Attorney, William L. Rynerson be relieved and his records seized. Leverson believed that these men would destroy all records if given the chance.[8]

Leverson again wrote to Secretary Schurz on the same day, mentioned his letter to Hayes, and reported that Lincoln County Sheriff William Brady had conducted illegal searches in violation of the citizen's civil rights.[9]

On April 1, Leverson again wrote to President Hayes, reporting that Sheriff Brady and his deputy had been killed, shot from ambush by Billy the Kid and friends, and predicted more bloodshed would follow unless "the governor be at once removed [from office]." Leverson seldom failed to interject criticism of the governor.[10]

The next day, Leverson posted another lengthy epistle to Hayes going into minute detail about the happenings in Lincoln County and once again called for action.[11]

Late in March, Edward Thornton again wrote to Evarts and informed him that he had received additional information about the murder:

> With reference to my note of the 9th instant, relative to the murder of Mr. J. H. Tunstall, a British subject, near Lincoln, New Mexico, I have the honor to inform you that I have received a letter from that place, of the 16th instant, in which it is charged that the above mentioned crime was incited by the District Attorney of the Third Judicial District, and the murderers are being screened or attempted to be screened by the Governor of the Territory and the Judge of the District.
>
> Without pretending that these charges are well founded until they shall be supported by further proof, it seems to me to be a case which demanded prompt and searching investigation, and I am confident that the Government of the United States will not fail to give to the matter its early and serious attention.
>
> It appears that when the murder of Mr. Tunstall took place warrants for the arrest of the murderers were issued on sworn informations by John B. Wilson, a Justice of the Peace.
>
> By the enclosed copy of a translation of the record, it appears that Mr. Wilson was duly appointed a Justice of the Peace on the 14th of February, 1877, by the County Commissioners, who, as appears by the enclosed translation of the 40th Section of the Acts of the Legislative

Assembly of the Territory of New Mexico, 1875-76, page 28, authorized to make such appointments.

>Notwithstanding the apparent legality of the appointment, a Proclamation, copy of which I have the honor to enclose, has been issued by the Governor of the Territory, declaring that Mr. Wilson's appointment by the County Commissioners was illegal and void, and that all processes issued by him were void.

>It is therefore to be presumed that the warrants issued by Mr. Wilson for the arrest of the abovementioned murderers will have no effect, and if it be true that some of the United States authorities are in league with them, there seems to be but little prospect that the murders will be brought to justice unless the government of the United States should take energetic measures to ensure their capture and trial.[12]

As he had done previously, Evarts forwarded the letter to United States Attorney General Charles Devens. His letter is dated April 3:

>Referring to the communication addressed to you by this Department, under date of the 13th March, ultimo, in relation to the murder in New Mexico of Mr. J. H. Tunstall a subject of Great Britain, I have now the honor to address a copy of a further note and of its accompaniments upon the subject, from the British Minister at this Capital, and to invite your attention to his request that energetic measures may be taken to secure the arrest and conviction of the murderers.[13]

CAUSE AND EFFECT

On April 9, Acting Attorney General S. F. Phillips answered the inquiries in a letter to Secretary of State Evarts:

> I have the honor to acknowledge the receipt of your communication of the 13th of March last and the 3rd. inst., with their enclosures in relation to the murder in New Mexico of Mr. J. H. Tunstall, alleged to be a subject of Great Britain.
>
> Upon receipt of the first named communication I addressed a letter to the District Attorney for New Mexico in which I directed him to institute a thorough inquiry into the circumstances of the murder and to report promptly to me whether from the facts any steps can or should be taken by the Government in the matter. I have not yet received a reply, but I have taken other measures to have the subject thoroughly investigated than through the officers of this Department now in New Mexico.[14]

Phillips had not received a reply from New Mexico because Catron was a leader in the notorious Santa Fe Ring, a group of men who controlled the territory politically. Additionally, the Ring backed the men who killed Tunstall. Asking Catron to investigate the crime was like asking a defendant to serve on the jury. Phillips' decision to seek help from other than "the officers of this Department now in New Mexico" was probably due to the fact that he was getting nowhere through official channels. Who was John Henry Tunstall? Was he indeed a British subject (Phillips called him an alleged British Subject)? Was it true that he was killed by United States officials as the British maintained? Were the accounts contained in these letters true? Even if the letters were only partially true they still pointed out a less-than-desirable condition in the territory.

As it turned out, John Henry Tunstall was indeed a British subject. Born in London in 1853 and well educated, he came to North America in 1872 to work in the family's business in Victoria, British Columbia. He remained there until early in 1876 when he decided to move on. California was his first stop, then in the fall he traveled to Santa Fe and on to Lincoln County, where he settled early the next year. He bought a ranch and soon opened a mercantile store. Tunstall and McSween entered into the banking business with another supporter, John S. Chisum, famed Pecos Valley rancher.[15] These ventures were in direct competition with the established firm of Murphy-Dolan, known after March of 1877 as J. J. Dolan & Co.[16] which had the Santa Fe Ring's backing.

Soon after Tunstall's arrival in Lincoln, he discovered that the county was ruled politically and economically by Major Lawrence G. Murphy and the partners of the Murphy-Dolan firm. The county sheriff and his deputy were aligned with them, as were both the judge and the district attorney of the 3rd Judicial District. Murphy and company contracted with the government to supply beef to nearby Fort Stanton and the Mescalero Indian Reservation. They also dealt in land and serviced the needs of the local ranchers. Their business practices were not always straightforward (they were known to sell merchandise at high prices while giving producers very little for the goods taken in trade), so Tunstall thought he could assume a share of their business by charging fair prices and not cheating the small operators. Had he stuck to ranching, Tunstall might have survived, but in opening his store, he exposed himself to open hostility from the Murphy-Dolan clique.

When Acting Attorney General Phillips wrote to Secretary of State Evarts on April 9, 1878, he advised that, ".... I have taken other measures to have the subject thoroughly investigated...." "Other measures" was the appointment of Frank Warner Angel as a special investigator. He was to travel to New Mexico, make an impartial inquiry into several related issues, and report his findings.

4 THE INQUIRY

Attorney Frank Warner Angel arrived in the territory in early May. His first stop was Santa Fe where he headquartered at the Exchange Hotel.[17] During these first days in New Mexico, Angel called on Governor Axtell, District Attorney Catron, and others. He explained his mission on behalf of the Departments of Interior and Justice.

Simply stated, Angel was to investigate the death of John Tunstall and other matters of embarrassment to Washington, including official culpability in the incident, the land grant schemes in Colfax County, and alleged corruption of public officials particularly Axtell and Catron for Lincoln County. He chose to take on the most difficult and dangerous part of his task first. Although the problems in Lincoln County were complicated and confusing, Angel was determined to be fair, thorough, and persistent in his research. (The final report testifies to his unbiased and relentless pursuit.)

The Cimarron *News and Press* had greeted the investigator by printing a letter penned by Robert Widenmann:

> ...If the iron heel of the "ring" is to be removed from the necks of our people; if monopolies are to be broken; if the blighting,

> despotic and pernicious power and influence of officials in New Mexico are to be brought to an end and authoritatively exposed, the people must come to the front. Every man and woman in New Mexico, knowing the damaging facts against U.S. officials should disclose them now to Mr. Angel. ... The administration has sent Mr. Angel to hunt the cause; the people who are familiar with the game must now guide the hunter...[18]

All editorials in the Territorial papers were not so favorable to the inspector, however, as is apparent in these excerpts from the Santa Fe *New Mexican*, a pro-Governor Axtell newspaper:

> This man has now commenced playing the role of informer and mud dauber, misrepresenting and perverting facts....You are now known, your dirty acts are known, and your blackmailing proclivities are known...[19]

The *New Mexican* referred to Angel as "Mr. Sleeve Buttons" recounting ugly gossip that a few years before, Angel had been accused of accepting bribes for his influence with Washington. The Las Vegas *Gazette* of May 18 cautioned Angel that he might "...get his wings shot off, or take his departure prematurely for the New Jerusalem..." The same newspaper warmly suggested that "...United States officials and all others in high places should be investigated about once a year, or oftener, if practicable."[20]

Despite what the local newspapers stated, Frank Angel was well qualified for the challenging task laid before him. Born in New York in 1845, he entered the Free Academy of the City of

New York in 1864. Angel graduated with 28 other students on July 2, 1868, with a bachelor of arts degree and was admitted to the New York State Bar in 1869. At the time of his visit to the Southwest, he was engaged in private practice from an office located at 62 Liberty Street, New York City. Angel already had gained valuable experience through several other detailed inquires performed for the federal government.[21]

Arriving in the small town of Lincoln in mid-May, Angel methodically began work taking over 300 legal-sized pages of testimony from anyone knowing anything about the death of Tunstall or the lawlessness abounding in the county. He interviewed people from both sides of the conflict; men who had ridden with the group that killed Tunstall, businessmen, lawmen, farmers, and those who supported the Tunsall-McSween side of the disturbance. Throughout late May and into early June, Alexander McSween took it upon himself to be Angel's guide and procurer of knowledgeable persons. On June 5, McSween wrote to Tunstall's father in England giving details of the federal probe:

> ...For the past week or ten days I have been very busy in taking testimony. Parties for years in the employ of Murphy have testified that sentence of death had been passed on your son and myself long before he was killed...One man testified that the Murphy & Co. party...offered him $1,000 if he would kill me....
>
> I have no doubt but that the United States government as a result of this investigation will be obliged to award you a large sum for your son's death. The testimony will be as full as it can be made....[22]

On June 11, Robert Widenmann wrote the elder Tunstall:

> ...Mr. Angel who is now engaged in investigating the conduct of officials in this territory seemed rather disgusted with their proceedings when I last saw him. May he prove an angel to us not only in name but also in deed.[23]

Montague R. Leverson, always outspoken, wrote several letters mentioning the investigation:

> Mr. Angel...has impressed me most favorably, and inspired me with great confidence both in his ability and integrity. They will murder him [Angel]...to prevent his report [from] reaching Washington...how much more desperate will be the measures resorted to, to get rid of Mr. Angel & his report.[24]

Angel himself told of the roadblocks placed in his path during the investigation. On October 3, he stated in a letter to the Secretary of the Interior, Carl Schurz, that he had been "...met by every opposition possible by the United Sates officials, and every obstacle thrown in my way by them to prevent a full and complete examination..."[25]

By late June, Angel had sufficiently analyzed the situation in Lincoln County and advised McSween to leave town and to go into hiding for the protection of his life.[26] Angel felt that the climate was ripe and that sooner or later, McSween would fall victim to the deadly plans of his opponents.

While in the southern part of the territory, Angel stumbled upon what he suspected to be fraud on the Mescalero Apache Reservation located a few miles from Lincoln. He evidently felt that this alleged wrongdoing demanded examination since he was also representing the Department of the Interior. He attended several issue days at the agency to watch the proceedings, check the tally books, and review the contracts. Based on this firsthand knowledge, he filed a separate report which charged the Agent, Fredrick Godfroy, with mishandling of government funds and property.

After completing his investigation in Lincoln County, Angel returned to Santa Fe to discuss his finding with territorial officials. It is unfortunate that he was not able to interview all of the principals in the events leading to Tunstall's shooting as several had been killed before Angel arrived in the territory. Some were shot from ambush, others executed by mobs, and a few simply were not available for various reasons, some real and some fabricated.

Angel remained in Santa Fe for a few days but by the latter part of July he went to the Cimarron and Las Vegas area to probe the Colfax County problems. It was here that he incurred the wrath of the Governor and many other territorial officials. Rumors arose that the investigator believed the Governor to have plotted the murder of several persons and that other members of the government were implicated[27]. The pro-Axtell newspapers raged in favor of the Governor. Angel telegraphed Washington not to accept resignations from any federal official in the territory until his inquiry was complete and filed with department heads in Washington.[28]

The Colfax County troubles dated back to before the murder of Reverend F. J. Tolby in Cimarron Canyon on September 14, 1875. The infamous Santa Fe Ring of rumored corrupt territorial officials were implicated in the murder and cover-up. These men had strong connections in the East and especially, Washington, D. C. Mrs. Mary McPherson, a close friend of Tolby's, resided in Washington and first raised the issue of the murder with federal officials.

Tolby was not the only fatality in Colfax County. There were other murders and much violence to go along with the

Reverend's demise. The infamous Clay Allison, and Maxwell Land Grant Attorney Frank Springer, and others were involved and made their reputations during these anxious times.

As early as 1869, the railroads wished to make use of Raton Pass on the border between New Mexico and Colorado since this pass was key to a California route. Since the pass fell inside the huge Maxwell land Grant, there was money to be made if the politicians and corrupt individuals could just get control of the land. Greed started all the turmoil in Colfax County and it smoldered for several years. Since Angel was dispatched to the Territory any way because of the flaming feud taking so many lives in Lincoln County, the power-that-be in Washington asked him to look into the difficulties in the northern part of New Mexico as well. Angel spent a few weeks taking testimony in Cimarron and Las Vegas and talking with those knowledgeable of these matters. It was the evidence discovered in this area that supported the downfall of several Territorial officials.

On the 11th of August, Angel presented Governor Axtell with a list of questions regarding his involvement in the difficulties besetting the area and demanded answers within 24 hours. Axtell was stunned. He asked for more time to respond, and Angel finally relented, giving him 30 days in which to comply.

Angel left for New York on the 14th.[29] He reached home on the 24th and began to sort, organize, and compile the enormous volume of paper collected out West. Now he faced the arduous task of editing the reports and drafting the letters that detailed his conclusions.

L. G. Murphy and Company: This photo was taken before the start of the Lincoln County War. (l to r) James J. Dolan, Colonel Emil Fritz, William Martin, Major Lawrence G. Murphy. (Courtesy of the Old Lincoln County Memorial Commission)

Rutherford B. Hayes, President of the United States: The President became involved in the Lincoln County troubles when locals petitioned his office for assistance. (Courtesy of the Library of Congress)

5 THE BATTLE

Troubles in Lincoln County had been brewing for several years but Tunstall's arrival started the rapid escalation. Over the few months before his death, the level of turmoil and disorder rose rapidly. Men were swearing out warrants against each other, the few merchants were at each other's throats, and cattle and horses were rustled daily.

Then the killings started. Shortly after Tunstall's slaying, on March 9, William Morton and Frank Baker were killed by a posse headed by Tunstall supporter, Dick Brewer. These deaths were likely murder since the circumstances surrounding the acts were somewhat questionable. In the same medley, an innocent rancher by the name of William McCloskey also became a victim of the blaze of gunfire.

On March 13, Tom Hill was killed and Jessie Evans wounded while attempting to rob a sheep camp at Alamo Springs, near Tularosa.

On March 28, in the middle of Lincoln, William Bonney (Billy-the-kid) took a shot at Billy Matthews but fortunately he missed. The next day, more gunfire was heard on the dirt street that ran through the center of the village.

CAUSE AND EFFECT

On April 1, about mid-morning, County Sheriff William Brady and his deputy, George Hindman are gunned down on the street of Lincoln from ambush by Bill-the-kid and others.

On April 4, at Doc Blazer's mill, each side lost one member. Dick brewer was killed by Andrew L. (Buckshot) Roberts. Shortly afterward, Roberts received a fatal wound from Billy-the-kid and co. Roberts died a few hours later.

On April 29, Frank McNab is killed and Ab Sanders fatally wounded. The next day, George Coe wounds Charles Kruling.

On May 14, a Dolan cowboy is killed and two others wounded at a Dolan cow camp.

All during this time there are charges and counter charges, men are arrested on both sides by the other carrying warrants issued by questionable authorities. There were robberies, attachments of cattle, horses, and other property, but through it all, no one was tried and all were released or escaped from custody or otherwise set free. It was a time of terrible unrest and no one in the county was safe.

Shortly after Frank Warner Angel arrived in the village, he assessed the situation and warned McSween to leave Lincoln if he valued his life. The danger was so ominous that even a newcomer could not misread the signs. But McSween ignored Angel's advice and chose to fight. On the evening of July 14,[30] he marshaled his forces and invaded Lincoln. He divided them into three groups; one went to Montano's store which was across the street and east of his residence, another set up headquarters in Ellis' store at the far eastern edge of town, and the third established its position in his home.

Sheriff George Peppin was caught by surprise but because McSween did not press his advantage, Peppin was able to regroup and strategically place his men around the small town. Just east of McSween's and across the street from Montano's business stood a tall adobe tower called the *Torreon*, which originally had been constructed for protection against Indians. Peppin successfully placed marksmen there giving him control of the street and placing McSween's men at a disadvantage since it separated them. Failure to secure this structure was McSween's undoing.

Fighting for the next three days consisted primarily of one group sniping at the other. There was one very significant exception to this; Sheriff Peppin asked Colonel N. A. M. Dudley, Commander of nearby Fort Stanton, to loan him a cannon. Dudley refused but someone took a shot at the soldier carrying Dudley's reply. Although the trooper was not injured, the incident gave the colonel an excuse to enter the fracas. On July 17, the Army conducted an informal board of inquiry into the shooting incident. Evidence points to the fact that the board talked primarily to the Murphy-Dolan supporters so it is not surprising that they found McSween's forces guilty of firing the round.[31]

On the fifth day of hostilities, July 19,[32] Colonel Dudley moved on Lincoln. His column of soldiers, pulling a Howitzer and a Gatling gun, paraded down the village's main street and bivouacked directly across from Montano's store and between McSween's house and the Ellis place. Not a single military round was fired, although the troops' presence had an undeniable effect.

McSween's men posted in Montano's and Ellis' buildings knew that they could not fight the Army. Although not cowards, they rightly reasoned that they had been outdone. Six-shooters and rifles were no match for a Howitzer and a Gatling gun. The official Army position was that they were there only to protect innocent bystanders but the men in the two stores doubted Dudley's sincerity. So on they moved. Deliberately, they saddled their horses, crossed the river and disappeared. Peppin made a feeble attempt to stop them, but probably was satisfied just to see them leave. Now McSween and the men in his house with him were desperate; they had lost two-thirds of their support while the opposition had added the United States Army to their side.

The withdrawal of the two fighting groups, enhanced by the moral support of the Army, inspired Peppin's men to attack with new vigor. A first attempt to torch the McSween house failed but a second try succeeded. The people inside the house now faced a new threat -- fire. The house, mostly adobe, burned slowly. In addition, the wind retarded the spread of the flames.

Mrs. McSween left the house and pleaded with Colonel Dudley to intervene and save her husband and the men with him. Although the officer could see the hopelessness of their situation, he told her that there was nothing he, the Army, could do. She returned to the house but left again for good as darkness approached. It was unwise for her to remain.

The men inside devised their final strategy, credited to Billy the Kid. The Kid would lead two or three men in a mad dash for the river in back of the house. While everyone's attention was focused on them, McSween and the others could escape. After it was dark, Billy and his followers dashed for the river. They suffered one casualty, young Harvey Morris. But now McSween made another mistake: he waited too long to run. He was shot down in his own doorway, along with Vicente Romero and Francisco Zamora.[33]

Although McSween's death ended the fighting between the two factions that had kept Lincoln County torn apart for so long, hostilities continued for a long period. The two sides had fought too long to forget their difference overnight. Less than a month later, Morris Bernstein, an employee of the Mescalero Indian Agency, was killed as he challenged whom he thought to be horse thieves. Several ex-McSween supporters were among his killers.[34]

Just a little over a month after Bernstein was shot, another force began to leave its mark on the county. During September and October, a surreptitious and violent John Selman and his gang of freebooters, known as "Selman's Scouts," terrorized the small settlements and ranches up and down the Hondo Valley. People were robbed, women raped, and several young boys killed for no real reason. The scouts operated out of Seven Rivers (near what is now Artesia, New Mexico), and enjoyed a free reign until the citizens decided they had had enough. The lawlessness of the county worked to Selman's advantage until Juan Patron (leader of the native population) led the Lincoln County Riflemen against them. Although the volunteers were not successful, their intent was clear and the Selman party moved on, eventually ending up in west Texas around Fort Davis where they were brought down by the Texas Rangers. Selman himself however, escaped after a short imprisonment. Several years later, Selman shot and killed John Wesley Hardin in El Paso. At the time, Selman was, ironically, filling a lawman's position. It was not long after when Selman was killed by another peace officer, George Scarborough.

Months after the "Scouts" left the territory, Mrs. McSween filed charges against Colonel Dudley, Sheriff George Peppin, and others for the killing of her husband. She retained a one-armed attorney named Huston I. Chapman from Las Vegas to help her settle these claims.

On the night of February 18, 1879, exactly one year after Tunstall's death, the two factions decided it was time for peace. They met on Lincoln's main street for final settlement of the feud. Reportedly, each faction lined up on opposite sides of the street and after much threatening and cursing by both sides, Jessie Evans and Billy-the-kid faced each other in the center of the dirt trail. Evans threatened to kill Bonney on the spot but surprisingly, Billy refused to fight and offered better terms. After some more haggling, the two divided groups of killers agreed that not one of them would testify against the other, that there should be no more killings, and several other points.

After shaking hands on the agreement, they decided to have a few drinks to celebrate the new pact. While this festival was in full swing, they met Chapman on the street and began making sport of him. In the confrontation, Jessie Evans and James Dolan shot the lawyer and his clothes were set on fire. Some sources attribute the cause of the fire to the muzzle blasts,[35] but it is also likely that Chapman's body was doused with whiskey and burned to destroy the documents he was carrying. The body remained where it had fallen until late the next night until solders from Fort Stanton came to retrieve the body the next evening.

Killings continued long through the aftermath of the Lincoln County War. Billy the Kid was tracked down at Fort Sumner and shot by Pat Garrett in July, 1881[36]. Juan Patron was killed on April1, 1884[37]. Patron had been mostly neutral during the war but had made enemies nonetheless. Because Lincoln's atmosphere of lawlessness had become too much to endure, he had moved to the Las Vegas region where his wife had relatives. One night in a local tavern, a stranger shot him dead. Although it was six years after the flames had been quenched in Lincoln, many blamed the enemies he had made there for his death.

Meanwhile, Lincoln gradually reverted back to the sleepy little village it had once been, except for fewer people and more tombstones.

Alexander McSween: Partner of John H. Tunstall in the mercantile and banking business. He was killed while attempting to escape his burning house during the five-day battle. (Courtesy M. G. Fulton Collection, Special Collections, University of Arizona Library).

John S. Chisum: Cattle King of the Pecos: Chisum was Tunstall's bank partner. Chisum became one of the largest ranchers in the Territory, controlling some 200 miles along the Pecos River. (Courtesy Wikipedia)

6 THE CONCLUSIONS

DEPARTMENT OF JUSTICE

IN THE MATTER OF THE CAUSE AND CIRCUMSTANCES OF THE DEATH OF JOHN H. TUNSTALL A BRITISHSUBJECT

TO THE HONORABLE CHARLES DEVENS, ATTORNEYGENERAL

In compliance with your instructions to make careful inquiry into the cause and circumstances of the death of John H. Tunstall, a British Subject, and whether the death of said Tunstall was brought about through the lawless and corrupt conduct of United States Officials in the Territory of New Mexico, and to report hereon.

I have the honor to submit the following report in relation to the premises.

FIRST: As to the cause of the death of John H. Tunstall. Mr. John H. Tunstall, by his straight-forward and honest business transactions with the people of Lincoln County, New Mexico, (Testimony pp. 79, 276, 326) had almost overthrown a certain faction of said County who were plundering the people thereof (Testimony pp. 5, 6, 89, 190, 274,276, 281)

He had been instrumental in the arrest of certain notorious horse thieves (Testimony pp. 10, 192, 277). He had exposed embezzlement of Territorial officers (Testimony pp. 13, 14, 29, 73, 129). He had incurred the anger of persons who had control of the County, and who used that control for private gain (Testimony pp. 5, 6, 190, 240, 292, 303, 320). He had introduced honesty and square dealings in his business, (Testimony pp. 276), and to the enmity of these persons, can be attributed the only cause of his death (Testimony pp. 27, 28, 277, 287, 320, 326)

SECOND: As to the circumstances of his death An attachment had been obtained against the property of one Alexander A. McSween (Testimony pp. 33, 193)

It was claimed that said Tunstall was McSween's partner (Testimony pp. 254, [?])

The Sheriff in order to attach certain property viz: stock and horses, alleged to [belong] to McSween and Tunstall sent his dep[uty] to Tunstall's ranch to attach the same ([Tes]timony pp. 35, 209) --when said deputy [visited] said ranch and was informed that he [could] attach the stock and leave a person [with] it until the courts could adjudicate to [whom] the stock belonged (Testimony pp. 35, 19 [?], 196, 245, 298) -he left without attach[ing] said property, and immediately assem[bled] a large posse among (Testimony pp. 36, [212, ?]) whom were the most desperate outlaws of the Territory

(Testimony pp. 277, 291, ?) they again started for Tunstall's ranch, in the mean-time Mr. Tunstall had been informed of the action of the horses and started for Lincoln, the County seat. (Testimony pp. 38, 200, 224, 299).

Directly after Tunstall had left his ranch, the Deputy Sheriff and said posse arrived there, and finding that Tunstall had left with the horses, deputized W. Morton (Testimony pp. 209, 213) who selected eighteen men and started out ostensibly to capture the horses. After riding about thirty miles, they came up to Tunstall and his party with the horses, and commenced firing on them (Testimony pp. 202)--immediately Tunstall and his party left the horses and attempted to escape (Testimony pp. 39, 218, 308) -were pursued and Tunstall was killed some hundred yards or more from the horses.(Testimony pp. 327).

Who shot Tunstall will never be known but there is no doubt that Wm. S. Morton, Jesse Evans, and Hill were the only persons present and saw the shooting, and that two of these persons murdered him. (Testimony pp. 39, 40, 232, 286). For Tunstall was shot in two places-- in the head and breast. (Testimony pp. 1, 2, 3, 39, 40) Of these persons Evans and Hill had been arrested at the instigation of Tunstall (p. 10,).

They were at enmity with Tunstall and enmity with them meant murder. (Testimony p.287)

There was no object for following after Tunstall, except to murder him, for they had the horses (Testimony pp. 218, 223, 327) which they desired to attach before they commenced to pursue him and his party. These facts, together with the bitter feeling existing against Tunstall, by certain persons to whom he had become obnoxious (Testimony pp. 227), and the deputy allowing these notorious out-laws to accompany him (Testimony pp. 225, 230) lead me to the conclusion that John H. Tunstall was murdered in cold blood (Testimony p. 271), and was not shot in attempting to resist an officer of the law. (Testimony p. 228).

THIRD: Was the death of John H. Tunstall brought about by the lawless and corrupt action of the United States officials—

After diligent inquiry and examination of a great number of witnesses, I report that the death of John H. Tunstall was not brought about through the lawless and corrupt conduct of United States officials in the Territory of New Mexico.

All of which is respectfully submitted.

(signed) Frank Warner Angel

Special Agent[38]

So reads Frank Warner Angel's summation on the death of John Henry Tunstall. To analyze why he reached these conclusions it is necessary to reference the various pages of testimony cited in the body of his letter.

FIRST: "As to the cause of the death of John H. Tunstall."

When Tunstall arrived in Lincoln County, it was apparent to everyone who met him that he held family funds to invest and could afford any business venture that would increase his purse. It was not long before he had acquired a ranch, complete with a sizable herd of cattle. Dick Brewer, a neighboring rancher, was employed as part-time foreman. Tunstall was not satisfied with this single business activity and began to branch out into other areas of local commence.

In the face of Murphy's enterprises which held a monopoly over the county's mercantile businesses, government beef contracts, the sale of goods needed for the nearby Mescalero Indian Reservation, and the lending of money, Tunstall opened his own store and promised the citizens a fair price for both the goods they purchased and the crops they sold. Before this time, anyone who opposed "The House," as Murphy & Co. were known, was forced out of the county. The citizens finally had a choice, after several years of going deeper and deeper in debt to Murphy.

The native Mexican-American population, mostly farmers and small ranchers, were the people most threatened by Murphy's operations and it was this same group who benefited most from Tunstall's store. They were, however, unorganized and defenseless against the guns employed by "The House."

Tunstall and his new ally, Alexander A. McSween, together with John S. Chisum also opened the Lincoln County Bank planning to make loans available at reasonable interest. This action further widened the gap between the two parties. If given a chance to recover from domination and with a ready source of funds, even the Mexican-American element could prove dangerous to Murphy and his partners.[39]

Juan Patron states in his affidavit to Angel that "Murphy told me that they would have to get rid of McSween and Tunstall."[40] Florencio Gonzales said, "I have no doubt that the murder of John H. Tunstall was premeditated and designed by L. G. Murphy, J. J. Dolan, and J. H. Riley, commonly know as 'The House' and carried out by their tools."[41]

In August 1877, according to McSween, Jesse Evans and Tom Hill, gunmen employed by Murphy, stole several horses from Tunstall and McSween. It was through the insistence of Tunstall and Brewer that Sheriff William Brady finally arrested these men at Beckwith's Ranch near Seven Rivers. While they were lodged in Lincoln jail, Tunstall visited them and even supplied whiskey. Although Evans told Tunstall that he would never recover the horses and Tunstall retorted that Evans should be hung, the meeting apparently ended on good terms, possibly due to the bottle of spirits. Not long afterwards, Evans and Hill escaped. According to affidavits attached to Angel's report, they were armed with saws and knives to assure their freedom. There is little doubt that this assistance was supplied by their employers with the full knowledge of the Sheriff.[42]

Immediately after their escape, the pair traveled to Brewer's ranch where they stole horses, saddles, and guns which belonged to both Brewer and Tunstall. When McSween heard of the escape, he offered to raise twenty men to assist Sheriff Brady in re-capturing the thieves. Brady declined by saying, "I arrested them once and I will be damned if I am going to do it again. Hereafter, I am going to look after Brady's interests." A few days later, the Sheriff was informed that the wanted men were at "The House." Brady again, according to McSween, made no effort to arrest them.[43]

As to the misdealings of territorial officials, McSween testified that in September of 1877, James Dolan asked McSween if he could borrow $1,000 to help him over a rough financial spot. McSween secured the money from Tunstall and when he delivered it to Dolan, he asked the storekeeper why he did not get Sheriff Brady to give him more tax money. Dolan replied that he had already tapped that source for all that it was worth. McSween had long felt that instead of taxes received being deposited in the treasury, Brady and Dolan were using them to finance Dolan's business.

The January 26, 1878, issue of the Mesilla Valley *Independent* printed a letter written by Tunstall on January 18, which accused Brady and Dolan of conspiracy involving territorial tax funds. Even Governor Axtell had admitted in an address to the legislature that Brady was default in his payment of taxes from Lincoln County.

Dolan's response was printed in the Independent on February 2. He denied any wrongdoing in the scandal and claimed that he had not used any money belonging to the territory in his private affairs.

As a result of this newspaper sparring, Dolan tried on February 6 to provoke Tunstall at Shedd's Ranch on the eastern slope of the Organ Mountains near Las Cruces. Tunstall, McSween, and others were camped at the ranch along with Deputy Sheriff Adolph P. Barrier of San Miguel County. Also camped nearby were some of Dolan's gunmen—Jessie Evans, Frank Baker, James J. Longwell, and John Long. Sometime during the night, Dolan arrived. Early the next morning, Dolan and Evans approached and when close enough for effective fire, Dolan cocked his Winchester and pointed it at Tunstall's breast, saying, "You damned coward. I want you to fight and settle our difficulties." Tunstall refused to fight. Finally, Deputy Sheriff Barrier stepped between the two men and slowed the action.

Dolan backed away shouting, "You won't fight this morning, you damned coward, but I'll get you soon." After he had retreated about 20 yards, Dolan made his parting comment: "When you write the *Independent* again say that I am with 'The Boys'." The term "The Boys" was used in Lincoln to denote a gang of thieves and murderers such as Evans, Baker, and others of Dolan's men.[44]

Therefore, Angel concluded that it was because of Tunstall's business dealings and his attempt to undermine the established monopoly that he was eliminated.

SECOND: "As to the circumstances of his death."

Alexander A. McSween had been retained to settle the estate of Colonel Emil Fritz by his two heirs, Emilie Scholand and Charles Fritz. The late colonel had been an early partner of Murphy's, but had sold out and returned to his homeland, Germany, before his death. He left a $10,000 insurance policy that McSween had been hired to collect. Murphy claimed that Fritz was still in debt to his company and had taken action to collect the money as part payment. Now that Dolan had taken over the operation of the store, it fell his duty to secure the funds.

Dolan convinced the heirs that McSween was dishonest, saying that he had collected and spent their money. Therefore, the plaintiffs, Emilie Scholand and Charles Fritz, requested the Third Judicial District Court to issue a writ of attachment against McSween's property. The writ was dated February 7, 1878.[45]

According to James Longwell, Tunstall testified in court that Alexander McSween was his business partner, and because of this association, it was unclear to the law what part of their property was jointly owned.[46] Therefore, Brady set out to take charge of all their holdings. He attached Tunstall's store in Lincoln and sent Jacob B. (Billy) Mathews with a posse to Tunstall's ranch to do the same with whatever stock he might locate.

McSween testified that he was not Tunstall's partner but rather his attorney. For his legal services, McSween was to have received one-half the profits of Tunstall's enterprises after the latter subtracted eight per cent as interest on the funds he had invested.[47] Nevertheless, Brady interpreted that agreement as a partnership, probably at Dolan's direction.

Mathews left Lincoln on February 9 to attach Tunstall's cattle. With him were John Hurley and Manuel Segoiva. Along the way, he was joined by Andrew L. "Buckshot" Roberts and George W. Hindman. After the posse passed the Mescalero Indian Agency, they were united with Frank Baker, Jessie Evans, Tom Hill, and John Long, alias "Rivers." Mathews denied that these four men were a part of his posse. They just merged with the lawmen and rode along with them. It is known that they were all acquainted and all worked for Murphy and Dolan from time to time.

Arriving at Tunstall's ranch on the Feliz River, they were met by about a dozen ranch hands.[48] Apparently Dick Brewer was willing for Mathews to tally the herd and leave one man to guard the cattle until the courts could decide to whom they belonged;[49] however, Robert Widenmann adamantly refused to allow Mathews to even approach the stock, let alone attach them. This caused Mathews to reconsider and he returned to Lincoln for counsel.

Upon hearing of Widenmann's steadfast refusal, Brady instructed Mathews to return, and this time, make sure he tallied the stock and supervised it until the courts convened. While camped at Paul's ranch on the return trip, Mathews was again joined by Hill, Evans, Baker, and Long. Again, Mathews claimed that they were not invited and were not officially part of his lawful body. Here, the posse was also met by several men from the Pecos country. With the posse now complete, they proceeded to Tunstall's. Although Mathews said that he ordered Hill and the others away, they accompanied the party. Unknown to Mathews, Tunstall had arrived at the ranch late the night before after hearing that the posse was reroute. He told his hands that he wanted no bloodshed and that at sunup they would take his horses into Lincoln and leave the cattle for Mathews. By the time the posse arrived, Tunstall and everyone else except Gauss, the cook, and Dutch Martin (Martin Martz) were gone, trailing the mounts to the village. These two were left to tell Mathews that the cattle were his.

At this point, Mathews split his party into two groups. One stayed with him to care for the cattle. He deputized William Morton to lead the other in overtaking the horses and returning them to the ranch.[50] Morton was told, according to Mathews, that only in the case of resistance was he to arrest the cowboys driving the herd.

Godfrey Gauss stated that as Morton was preparing to leave the ranch to catch up with Tunstall and the horses, he yelled to the others, "Hurry up boys, my knife is sharp and I feel like scalping someone." Gauss said that the entire posse seemed excited and acted as though they wanted to kill someone. Henry Brown, who left Tunstall's ranch on the morning of the 18th, and happened upon the posse a few miles from the ranch, said that he was told by Morton and Baker that they were going to kill somebody at the ranch.

After riding hard for several hours, the posse caught sight of the slow moving horse herd about 5:30 p.m. At this point the story varies depending on whom one takes as an authority. Persons associated with Murphy and Dolan stated that Tunstall was killed while resisting arrest. Those close to the Tunstall—McSween side of the fracas said that he was murdered in cold blood.

Angel's remarks about the details of the death were taken from the affidavits of Pantelon Gallegos, John Middleton, Alexander McSween, Robert Widenmann, and Florencio Gonzales. Gallegos and Middleton represented the Tunstall side and the others supported the Murphy-Dolan interests. From these affidavits, it is somewhat surprising that Angel concluded that Tunstall was killed as he ran. Middleton, for instance, says that as they fled, he yelled for Tunstall to follow but the Englishman hesitated, saying, "What, John? What, John?" After the drovers topped the hill, Tunstall gave up his sidearm and was deliberately shot in the breast by Evans. Tunstall fell on his face and was then shot in the back of the head by Morton using Tunstall's own pistol. Morton then killed the dead man's horse, again with Tunstall's revolver.

McSween quoted Thomas Green who reportedly told him that Tunstall gave his pistol to Morton and was subsequently shot in the breast by Evans. Gallegos states that as they topped a hill in back of the horse herd, he saw a man on a grey mount (several others said Bonney was the only one riding a grey; everyone else was mounted on bays) yell something to the men at the head of the horses, but that he was too far away to hear the words. The posse then charged the others and became strung out, with many falling quite a ways behind. The leaders of the posse, Morton, Evans, and

Hill, went out of sight ahead of the remainder. Shots were heard and Morton came back into view saying that Tunstall had shot at him and all three posse men returned the fire, killing Tunstall.

When the shooting stopped, Tunstall's saddle horse was rounded up and shot. The dead man's hat was placed under the animal's head, Tunstall's head was put on his rolled up overcoat, and the body was put on a blanket with another thrown over the top. The attackers then rode back to the ranch where Mathews and the others were counting cattle.

Gonzalez states that the body was recovered some 100 yards from the trail. This indicates that he may have attempted to take flight before he was shot. Angel accepts this view. From reading the slightly different accounts contained in affidavits not cited by Angel, it can only be stated with some certainty that Tunstall's drovers did run for cover at the first sight of the firing group of men. Tunstall also may have attempted escape, only to be shot down 100 yards from the trail. Or discovering he had been abandoned, simply waited for the men to gallop up, surrendered his weapon, and then had taken bullets in the chest and head. It is unlikely that he would have first elected not to run and then, vastly outnumbered and at close range, tried to shoot it out with men having much more frontier savvy.

Since everyone with the possible exception of Tunstall had left the horses they were driving, and these animals were the property the posse desired, Angel concludes that they could have been easily secured; therefore the only reason for pursuing Tunstall was to kill him. This fact together with the bitter feeling existing against Tunstall by "notorious outlaws" who were riding with the posse, led Angel to the theory that Tunstall was murdered in cold blood,[51] not while resisting an officer of the law.[52]

As Angel noted in his conclusions, which man or men shot Tunstall will never be known but it is certain that it was one or two of three men: William Morton, Tom Hill, or Jessie Evans. These were the only three that were within sight of him when the shooting occurred. Two of them did not live long enough to make a statement. Before the special agent arrived in the territory,

William Morton and Frank Baker were killed near Blackwater Canyon by members of the Tunstall-McSween clan. They had been arrested in early March, and while being transported to Lincoln, were killed by Billy the Kid, Dick Brewer, John Middleton, and others, reportedly while trying to escape.

A few days later, Hill was killed by a half-breed Cherokee Indian tending a sheep camp that Hill and Evans tried to rob. In the same melee, Evans was wounded but managed to escape. Evans' injury eventually landed him in the Fort Stanton hospital just a few miles from Lincoln. He remained there throughout Angel's investigation in the Lincoln County area; nevertheless, there is no indication that Angel attempted to extract a statement from him. While it is possible that the taking of a deposition was attempted by Angel, no where does the special Agent note that he endeavored to talk with him nor does he acknowledge being refused an interview.

Evans did make a statement to Indian Inspector E. C. Watkins which is contained in the portion of Angel's report on fraud at the Mescalero Reservation. The information in this affidavit does not mention the Tunstall episode nor the Lincoln County troubles in general. It only discusses animals taken from the Agency by Evans and others in years past while in the employ of John S. Chisum. Since Evans was the only man alive at the time of Angel's investigation who saw and was involved in Tunstall's murder, it is unfortunate that we do not have his views recorded; even though their validity would have to be questioned.

THIRD: "Was the death of John H. Tunstall brought about by the lawless and corrupt action of United States officials--"

After mulling over voluminous evidence gathered, Frank Angel reasoned that, although Tunstall was surely murdered, it was not caused by the illegal conduct of United States officials in the Territory of New Mexico.

7 THE RESULTS

Soon after Angel arrived in New York and began to compile his final report, he was urgently summoned to Washington by the President. Hayes was impatient to hear the details of Angel's investigation and would not wait for the official report to be prepared. Instead he had Angel give him a verbal report of the findings.

Only a few days after returning to his home, Angel was again requested to come to Washington. He had learned that General Lew Wallace of Civil War fame and Indiana Republican politician, was soon to become Axtell's successor as governor of the territory. Among other wrongdoings, Axtell had been accused of plotting to kill Frank Springer of Cimarron and others. His actions during the Lincoln County War also demanded that he be replaced.

It was important that Wallace understand who supported whom, who could be trusted, and the character of the people involved in the New Mexico troubles. In a meeting with Angel, he produced a red leather, pocket-sized notebook in which Angel recorded his assessment of the personalities that the governor would encounter. Angel also included critical comments of the existing newspapers in the territory. Undoubtedly, the document was studied by the new leader on his way west.[53]

Angel's visit to the White House bore other fruit as well. In late September, Fredrick Godfroy resigned as Indian Agent of the Mescalero Apache Reservation. When the final report arrived in Washington, it provided a clear understanding as to why Godfroy chose to quit.

Although Angel felt that Godfroy was guilty of mishandling government funds and property, he went to great lengths to express the positive acts that had transpired on the reservation since Godfroy assumed command. Godfroy's daughter had taught many Indians, both young and old, "to love and fear God," and she was teaching the Indians to read and write. The affidavits collected by Angel lent support to and confidence in Godfroy's influence over his wards. The depredations had all but ceased, and the welfare of the Indians was better than ever.

There was, however, considerable evidence supplied that Godfroy had loaned up to 13,000 pounds of government property to private individuals. He had misrepresented the number of Indians on the reservation and issued many times more goods than required. By actual count, Angel found 373 Indians in residence. Also there was Godfroy's close association with the Murphy-Dolan faction of the conflict. This federation certainly did not enhance his cause.

In view of the conflicting testimony and his personal feelings in the matter, Angel pleaded that Godfroy be given sufficient time to resign rather than face criminal charges. His recommendation carried considerable weight with the Department of the Interior, and the agent's resignation was requested.[54]

While investigating Indian agents, Angel researched Doctor B. M. Thomas, Agent of the Pueblo Indians. Doctor Thomas was also charged with misappropriation of government funds and property. These wrong actions were alleged to have been for his personal gain and private use. Angel concluded that Thomas should be given the benefit of the doubt since he was a Christian man, had done many things to help the Indians, and there were only two persons who testified to his fraud while several of Santa Fe's respected citizens swore to the agent's honesty.

There was one other incident of which Thomas admitted his guilt. Although he owned his home, he had obtained vouchers stating that he was renting, and had submitted these to the department for payment, explaining that he thought it was the custom within the Indian department. Once informed of this being fraudulent, he became remorseful. Angel recommended that, although the action was illegal, it should be considered only censurable and the doctor should remain in the service of the Bureau of Indian Affairs.[55]

As for United States Attorney, Thomas B. Catron, Angel concluded that he was probably guilty of misusing his office for personal gain and being a leader of the famous Santa Fe Ring. Angel gave Catron a chance to answer the charges made against him; however, after several requests for an extension, Catron chose to tender his resignation rather than respond. On October 10, 1878, he did so, and was replaced a few weeks later.[56]

The main chore of the investigation was to determine if Tunstall was killed as a result of misconduct by united States officials. To this Angel responded that he was not. Nevertheless, the Tunstall family in England continued to request reparations from the United States government. For many years after, letters were exchanged across the Atlantic addressing the causes of the murder. Finally, on January 7, 1886, the British Foreign Office informed the Tunstall clan that it had received a communiqué from the United States Secretary of State, "...that after a full review of the facts and circumstances, the Government of the U.S. could not admit any liability as attaching to it in relation to the case either directly towards the representatives of the murdered man or internationally, towards Her Majesty's Government, demanding in their behalf...Lord Salisbury regrets, therefore, to have to inform you that no further steps can be taken in the matter."[57]

After eight years, the case was closed. Both the British government and the Tunstall family had given up their claim. Even though Angel's report had been filed with Her Majesty's government, and the elder Tunstall had studied it at length, it took a long time to refute the accusations.

CAUSE AND EFFECT

Thomas B. Catron: United States Attorney for the Territory until he resigned due to Angle's report findings. (Courtesy Museum of New Mexico)

8 THE LATER YEARS

How did the principals who survived the conflict spend their later years? For some, their fighting was over; for others, they died as they lived--violently.

FRANK WARNER ANGEL

After completing his report to Washington, Angel returned to private practice in New York City. He was, for many years, the Assistant District Attorney of Brooklyn. Moving to Jersey City, he was appointed Fire Commissioner by Mayor Fagan on January 1,1902, as a Republican. In 1903, he transferred to become the Commissioner of Appeals for the regulation of tax assessments. On January 1, 1906, poor health, which had plagued Angel for nearly two years, forced him to leave the Board of Appeals. He retired to his home at 820 Whiton Street where he succumbed at 5:30 a.m. on March 15, 1906. Angel was survived by his wife, Sadie, and one daughter, Mrs. Van Dien. Internment was in Greenwood Cemetery on Saturday, March 17.

SAMUEL B. AXTELL

Surprisingly, only four short years after being replaced as territorial governor, on August 1, 1882, Axtell was appointed Chief Justice of the Territory of New Mexico. He held this office until he resigned in 1885. President Arthur's appointment of Axtell to the New Mexico Supreme Court aroused many protests concerning his past; nevertheless, he kept the position. After retiring from the bench, Axtell continued to live in Santa Fe. He died on August 6, 1891, while visiting relatives in Morristown, New Jersey and was buried there.

WILLIAM BONNEY, ALIAS "BILLY THE KID"

Bonney remained on the run in Lincoln County after the war and continued his lawless ways. He was subsequently captured by Sheriff Pat Garrett, tried and sentenced to hang for the ambush murder of Sheriff William Brady on April 1, 1878 on the streets of Lincoln. Bonney then made his famous escape from the Lincoln county Courthouse (which was, ironically, once the Murphy-Dolan store), killing two guards in the process. A few months later, on the night of July 14, 1881, he slipped into Pete Maxwell's house in Fort Sumner. Unknown to him, Sheriff Pat Garrett had entered only minutes before. Gun-play ensued and Billy was killed. He was buried the next day in the Fort Sumner cemetery.

THOMAS B. CATRON

Catron continued in politics in spite of being forced to resign as U.S. Attorney. He was elected to the Territorial Legislature four times, served on the Santa Fe Board of Education, and was at one time the Mayor of Santa Fe. In 1912, Catron was elected to the United States Senate where he served until 1917. He died in his beloved Santa Fe on May 21, 1921. Catron County, in western-central New Mexico bears his name today.

JOHN S. CHISUM

Chisum continued to ranch at South Spring River Ranch until his death in December 1884. A tumor in his neck slowed him late in life and in the summer before his death, he journeyed to Kansas City to undergo surgery, but before he could return to the territory, the trouble reappeared. Doctors refused to attempt additional operations so Chisum traveled to Eureka Springs, Arkansas in the hopes that the mineral baths would provide a cure; nevertheless, his condition was terminal. The body was taken to Paris, Texas for burial in the family plot.

JAMES J. DOLAN

The war brought financial ruin to Dolan, and before its close, he had been forced to sell out. Just a year later, he married Caroline Fritz, heir to the Emil-Fritz estate. Ironically, Dolan took over the former Tunstall property and reentered the mercantile business in the former Tunstall store. The ranch on the Rio Feliz became the Dolan family home. Although he became financially solvent in the cattle business, politics were his special forte. He served as County Treasurer for five years, and was then elected to the Territorial Senate. He was later appointed to the Federal Land Office at Las Cruces for two years. Dolan died on February 26, 1898, and was buried in the Fritz family plot along the Rio Bonito below Lincoln even though he had married Maria Eva Whitlock in 1886 after Caroline's death.

JESSIE EVANS

Evans, the only person present at the scene of the Tunstall shooting, survived the Lincoln County War and contrary to Billy-the-kid, he fled the Territory and went to Texas. There, his outlaw ways continued and he eventually was involved with the shooting death of a Texas Ranger. That landed him in the Texas Prison in

Huntsville in 1880. Evans went over the wall in 1882 and has never been heard from again. Did he live to a ripe old age sitting in a rocking chair? Somehow that seems doubtful. He never, in his recorded history showed the slightest suggestion of going straight. While it is possible that he left Texas and lived a lawful life under an assumed name, it is probable that he drifted into trouble somewhere else in the West and fell victim to a lawman's bullet and now lies unknown in a pauper graveyard, without his recollection of Tunstall's killing untold.

FREDERICK C. GODFROY

Frederick C. Godfroy was born in Monroe, Michigan in 1828. He attended the University of Michigan but did not obtain a degree. He was a store and bank clerk for awhile, married Clara Philips on December 1, 1849, served as town marshal and collector in 1854, was the assessor for the 3rd. Ward in 1860, and served as City Recorder from 1862-1864.

In July, 1876, he was appointed as Indian Agent at the Mescalero Reservation a few miles from Lincoln. After Angel identified his fraudulent ways in 1878, Godfroy was allowed to resign in early September, 1878 and sink into historical oblivion. He died in New York State on June 15, 1885 and was interred in Buffalo.

LAWRENCE. G. MURPHY

Murphy transferred his interest in "The Big House" to J. J. Dolan in March of 1877 and the establishment thereafter became known as J. J. Dolan and Company. In May of the same year, Murphy named Dolan as sole beneficiary in his will. This probably indicates that there was still some financial interest between Murphy and Dolan but what the connection was is unknown. Murphy moved to Santa Fe on May 6, 1878, likely fleeing the aftermath of Tunstall's killing. Murphy never returned to Lincoln County and was henceforth a non-player in the conduct of the War. Murphy died on October 20, 1878, reportedly of alcoholism.

According to Frank Coe, Murphy was sick when he relocated to Santa Fe and immediately entered the Sisters of Charity Hospital. Apparently the sisters cut off his drink and he succumbed a few months later.

ROBERT WIDENMANN

Robert Widenmann shook the Lincoln County dust off his boots in mid-June when he traveled to Dona Ana County to testify in court—he never set foot in Lincoln County again. Widenmann was reared in Ann Arbor, Michigan, the son of the Bavarian Consul. He traveled west and arrived in Lincoln in February, 1877. He soon became friendly with the Tunstall-McSween cause, and with his father's help, he obtained an appointment as a Deputy United States Marshall. Although Widenmann carried warrants for the arrest of Jessie Evans, he refused to try and serve them. Never considered to be a formidable gunfighter by early western standards, he seems to have held a vivid recollection of his ability on the frontier. In his later years, in Ann Arbor, he is reported to have spent many hours in the family orchard practicing his fast draw and pistol shooting. Robert Widenmann died on April 15, 1930.

APPENDIX A – LINCOLN COUNTY REPORT DESCRIPTION

Angel's report on the death of John Tunstall, as deposited with the National Archives consists of two files. One contains mostly correspondence pertaining to the troubles in New Mexico Territory. The second is a massive collection of affidavits taken by Angel and others. These testimonies provided the information from which Angel drew his conclusions concerning the causes and details of Tunstall's murder.

The Correspondence File

The correspondence file contains 171 pages of mostly handwritten, legal-size letters. There is a smattering of newspaper articles contributed by persons in the territory, a few document copies that are typed and several telegrams to and from territorial and federal officials.

A collection of letters to the State Department from the British Minister asking what the United States government was doing about the death of a British subject on the American frontier. Enclosures with these letters defended John B. Wilson as a Justice of the Peace in Lincoln County. There had been some contention that Wilson was not a legally appointed officer, and the British Minister endeavored to bring the particulars of the matter to light by enclosing a translation from Spanish of the February 14, 1877, appointment of Wilson as Justice of the Peace.

Also, included for the enlightenment of federal officials, was a copy of Governor Axtell's March 9, 1878 Proclamation to the citizens of Lincoln County. It reads:

> The disturbed conditions of affairs at the county seat brings me to Lincoln County at this time. My only object is to assist good citizens to uphold the laws and to keep the peace. To enable all to act intelligently it is important that the following facts should be clearly understood.
>
> 1st John B. Wilson's appointment by the County Commissioners as a Justice of the Peace was illegal and void, and all processes issued by him were void, and said Wilson has no authority whatever to act as Justice of the Peace.
>
> 2nd The appointment of Robert Widenmann as U. S. Marshall has been revoked, and said Widenmann is not now a peace officer, nor has he any power or authority whatever to act as such.
>
> 3rd The President of the United States upon an application made by me as Governor of New Mexico, has directed the Post Commander Col. Geo. A. Purington to assist Territorial Civil officers in maintaining order and enforcing legal process. It follows from the above statements of facts that there is no legal process in this case to be enforced, except the writs and processes issued out of the Third Judicial District Court by Judge Bristol, and there are no Territorial Civil officers here to enforce these, except Sheriff Brady and his deputies.

Now, therefore, in consideration of the premises, I do hereby command all persons to immediately disarm and return to their homes and usual occupations, under penalty of being arrested and confined in jail as disturbers of the Public Peace.

S. B. Axtell

Governor of New Mexico

Lincoln, March 9, 1878

Section 40 of the Acts of the Legislative of the Territory of New Mexico, 1875-1876, page 28, written in Spanish, was also forwarded. This document states that when the position of any county official becomes vacant, the county commissioners shall have the power to fill such vacancy, the County Commissioners shall have the power to fill such vacancy by appointment until the next election. Nevertheless, Axtell had removed Wilson and Widenmann and had bolstered himself with the Murphy-Dolan faction by reaffirming Brady as the lawful authority.

This file contains many letters describing conditions in Lincoln County prior to and after Tunstall's death. Montague R. Leverson wrote two letters to President Hayes telling his version of the causes of the trouble. Although somewhat biased, these letters provide an outside view by a newcomer to the area.

There are letters to the government from Henry M. Arms, Robert Widenmann, W. Haskell, and the commander of Fort Stanton, Colonel N. A. M. Dudley who took over from Purington on March 26, 1878. All give their views on the civil uprising in the county. Dudley encloses an affidavit by George Peppin, who reigned as sheriff after Brady's murder. Peppin tells of the conditions in Lincoln after the July battle, asks for help from the military, and discusses the shooting death of the Indian Agency clerk, Morris J. Bernstein.

Pertaining to Thomas Catron, there are 38 pages of data. Most are letters from Catron seeking additional time to answer the charges brought against him by Angel. There are an equal number of replies from the federal government refusing to grant the extension. And there is also a copy of Catron's resignation as United States Attorney of New Mexico Territory.

Several telegrams from U.S. Marshall John Sherman request aid from the military in capturing criminals. He also asks for money to employ two detectives to chase banditti who fled to Colorado. The reply--no funds.

A copy of the indictment of William Bonney and others for the slaying of Andrew L. "Buckshot" Roberts is included. Roberts was killed at Blazers Mill shortly after Tunstall's death.

The letters from Angel are stored in this section: "In the matter of the Lincoln County Troubles" to Charles Devens (see Chapter 1), and "In the matter of the cause and circumstances of the death of John H. Tunstall a British subject" also to Devens (see Chapter 6).

The Affidavits Section

The affidavits section of the report contain the various statements made by persons knowledgeable of the affair and these are the pages referenced in Angel's letter on the cause of John Tunstall's demise. By actual count the file contains 346 pages; although Angel's numbering goes to 392. Either there are 46 pages now missing or Angel decided not to include some affidavits in his final submission. From Angel's index, it cannot be determined what might be lacking. There is, however, some indication that the report has been tampered with through the years.

CAUSE AND EFFECT

In his book, *The Life and Death of John Henry Tunstall*, Frederick W. Nolan states, "that the records had been removed earlier by Secretary of War, Stephen Elkins, during the tenure of President Garfield." While this cannot be substantiated, it should be known that Elkins had at one time been a law partner of Thomas Catron, and it was said that "Elkins takes care of Washington and Tom Catron looks after New Mexico."

In 1892, Catron was still worried about the effects of Angel's report on his political future (see "*The Great New Mexico Cover-up*," Norman Cleveland, *Rio Grand History*). In September of that year, Catron wrote to Elkins in Washington stating that "...the democrats are desirous to obtaining a copy of that man Angell's [sic] report against me...I wish you would see the Attorney General and see that he does not allow any copy of that paper to be issued to any one..."

In February, 1893, Catron was still not satisfied and asked Elkins to "get that report and destroy it." Catron referred to the document as "a piece of mudslinging." Elkins replied in March: "I have had a diligent search made for Angel's report...but it cannot be found."

From all indications, the report was buried in Washington and lay undiscovered for many years. The first known use of the report was by Maurice G. Fulton in the late 1940's and early 1950's while researching for his book *The Lincoln County War*. British author Frederick W. Nolan discovered part of a report in the British Foreign Office archives in the early 1950's. Mr. Donald Mosholder of the National Archives told the author in 1978 that he located the report several years before and at that time, the issue records indicated that very few persons had seen it since it was filed with the agency.

Nonetheless, the report as it now exists appears complete, except for Angel's page number discrepancy and the National Archives feels that this is exactly the condition in which it was submitted for their safekeeping.

Angel's affidavit index:

INFORMANT   PAGE

Appel, D. M.   1

Barrier, A. P.   289-185

Beckwith, R. A.   231

Brown, Henry   305

Bonney, W. H.   314

Baker, William   364

Cockran, Thomas   232

Dolan, James J.   235

Dowlin, William   365

Frederick, T. F.   363

Gallegos, P.   217

Gauss, G.   297

Gonzlaes, F.   324

Goodwin, J.   381-370

Galsen, J.   385

Hurley, John   260

Howe, A. H.   288

Kruling, Charles   265

Longwell, J. J.   248

Lust, H.   357

McSween, A. A.   342-5

Mathews, J. B.   209

Murphy, L. G.   256

Montano, J.   281

Middleton, J.   307

Martinez, A.   340-311

Newcomb, J.   322

Olinger, J. W.   229

Perry, S. R.   223

Patton, J.   271

Patron, J. B.   273

Purington, George A.   348

Peppin, G. W.   353

Robinson, B.   391-389

Shields, D. P.   185

Smith, G. W.   362

Sampson, C.   387

Vansickle, G.   320

Widenmann, R. A.   332-187

Daniel M. Appell's testimony concerns the postmortem examination of Tunstall's body. In the document, he describes in medical terms the two wounds, one in the chest and the other in the head, stating that either wound alone would have ended the man's life. Appel says that there were no powder burns on the body to indicate that the killing shots were fired closer than six feet.

The William Baker whose affidavit is included should not be confused with Frank Baker who rode with the Mathews' posse. Frank Baker was killed before Angel arrived in the Territory. William was a Private from Company H of the 9th Calvary at Fort Stanton. His squad had been dispatched to Lincoln after Tunstall's death to protect McSween and others.

McSween's two affidavits are by far the most comprehensive of all. They are comprised of 140 pages of handwritten, legal size paper, including 21 exhibits. These attachments consist of other persons' affidavits, legal documents, check copies (handwritten, and certified as true copies by the copier of the original), newspaper articles, business ledgers, a letter from the governor, letters from W. L. Rynerson, District Attorney, and various other writings.

It is apparent that McSween felt that he and Tunstall were in the right. Although he knew he was a marked man, the file does not indicate that he truly feared for his life. McSween told their side of the conflict from the beginning to early June 1878. Six weeks later, McSween lay dead at the doorstep of his home, felled by bullets from the guns of his adversaries.

APPENDIX B—CHARGES AGAINST GOVERNOR S. B. AXTELL

The following are Frank Warner Angel's conclusions concerning the charges against New Mexico Territorial Governor S. B. Axtell. Also included is the index of letters, statements, affidavits, proclamations, and documents collected during the investigation:

Interior Department

In the matter of the investigation of the charges

against

S. B. Axtel [Axtell], Governor of New Mexico

To the Honorable C. Schurz

Secretary of the Interior

--In compliance with your request made at the time I made my first report herein, I herewith make my supplemental and final report as to the charges against said S. B. Axtel

[Axtell]. Since making said report I have found no reason for changing the same -- but on the contrary believe as I did then that the best interests of New Mexico demanded the removal of S. B. Axtell as Governor --

-- A brief resume of the facts laid before you at that time will be necessary to make this report complete –

---Under your instructions I visited New Mexico for the purpose of ascertaining if there was any truth in the repeated complaints made to the Department as to fraud, in competency, and corruption of United States officials. I determined to see with my own eyes and hear with my own ears. I traveled over most of the Territory. I visited almost every important town and talked with the principal citizens thereof--

-- I was met by every opposition possible by the United States civil officials and every obstacle thrown in my way by them to prevent a full and complete examination with one exception and administration of affairs in the Territory and from facts coming under my observation and affidavits of the people the following charges in substance were made against the Governor of said Territory--

First

That the Governor had taken strictly partisan action as to the troubles in Lincoln County--

Second

That he refused to listen to the complaints of the people of that County--

Third

That he had been paid the sum of two thousand dollars to influence his action--

Fourth

That he arbitrarily removed Territorial officials thereby outlawing citizens, and usurping the functions of the judiciary—

Fifth

That he removed officials and in their place appointed strong partisans--

Sixth

That all action taken by him has increased rather than quieted the troubles in Lincoln County--

Seventh

That he appointed officials to office and kept them there who were supported by the worst out-laws and murderers that the Territory could produce--

Eighth

That he knowingly appointed bad men to office--

Ninth

That he was a tool of designing men Weak and arbitrary in exercising the functions of his office--

Tenth

That he was a Mormon and desired to turn the Territory into a Mormon settlement--

Eleventh

That he conspired to murder innocent and law abiding citizens because they opposed his wishes and were exerting this influence against him—

Twelfth

That he arbitrarily refused to restore the courts to Colfax County and refused to listen to the petitions of the people of that County for the restoration thereof--

--The Governor at first refused to be investigated preferring to ignore the complaints against him on the ground that the Department of the Interior had no power to investigate him (testimony p. 4). He has not even answered the charges by a sworn statement. I received just before making my first report, a newspaper article which was not even signed by him in reply to the charges against him--

--By much care and patience I have investigated the above charges impartially, seeking to obtain the truth and punish the guilty--

--Many things came to my notice and observations and of which no affidavits could be obtained. Many suspicious circumstances existed which convinced me beyond a peradventures that Gov. Axtell was an improper person for the place. He is a man of strong prejudices, impulsive, conceited, and easily flattered -- all these make a man easily influenced, a complete tool in the hands of designing men--

<u>As to the charges one and two,</u> I found Lincoln County convulsing by an internal war. I inquired the cause. Source one was responsible for the blood shed in that County. I found two parties in the field one headed by Murphy, Dolan and Riley—the other led by McSween-- both had done many things contrary to law -- both were violating the law-- McSween I firmly believe acted conscientiously -- Murphy, Dolan, & Riley for revenge and personal gain. The Governor came, heard the Murphy, Dolan, & Riley side, refused to hear the people who were with McSween or the residents of the County and acted strictly in advancing the Murphy, Dolan, and Riley party-- Murder and unlawful acts followed instead of peace and quiet which could have been accomplished if the Governor had acted as he should have done and listened patiently to both sides. The opportunity presented itself to him to have quieted and stopped the trouble in Lincoln Co.-- by his partisan action he allowed it to pass and the continuations of the troubles that exist today in Lincoln County are chargeable to him. He was a partisan either through corruption or weakness and charges first and second have been sustained.--

<u>Charge Third</u> The facts are that in May 1876, Gov. Axtell borrowed of Mr. Riley $1800 and it is alleged that the same was paid in November (testimony p. 7). I do not believe that Gov. Axtell received this money to directly influence his action. It was some time before the troubles actually commenced in Lincoln Co.- Although they were brewing at that time. The only influence this transaction could have on the

action of Gov. Axtel[l] was in as much as Riley had befriended him to return the compliment, and certainly his official action lays him open to serious suspicion that his friendship for Murphy, Dolan, and Riley was stronger than his duty to the people and the government he represents--

<u>Charge Forth</u> --I find that this charge has been freely sustained by his proclamation of March 9, 1878 (testimony p. 8). He usurped the functions of the judiciary and in fact removed J. B. Wilson, a Justice of the Peace, and thereby made certain persons who were in good faith enforcing the warrants issued by said Wilson outlaws (testimony p. 4). What right had he to do this? He did not veto the bill under which Wilson was appointed and suffered him to act some months before he arbitrarily removed him--

<u>Charge Fifth</u>--John Copeland after the murder of Sheriff Brady was appointed Sheriff. He was an honest, conscientious man, perhaps he was not the strongest man in character that ever existed--but I am yet to hear of any arbitrary act on his part any murder, robbery, arson in which he has been a party or of his being supported while in office by a band of notorious outlaws and nonresident. He was on the contrary surrounded by and had the confidence of a majority of the residents of the county—One of the County Commissioners his bondsman. By the laws of the territory, the Sheriff is ex-officio Tax Collector. The bonds as collector have to be fixed by the County Commissioners after they have ascertained the amount of taxes to be collected--Copeland had nothing to do with this--

and owing to the troubled state of affairs in the county, the County Commissioners could not find the amount of taxes to be collected.

The Governor immediately seized the opportunity to aid Murphy, Dolan, & Riley--He this time acts strictly within the letter of the law, and would that I could say the interest of the law and non-partisan--He removes Copeland and appoints G. W. Peppin, one of the leaders of the Murphy, Dolan, and Riley party--Who comes from Mesilla accompanied by John Kinney and his murderous outfit of outlaws, as a body guard to assist him in enforcing law and order--Again we have an unusual number of murders, robbers, and accompanied with arson, and after Kinney and his party have accomplished their mission of murdering McSween and robbing and stealing all they can they retire on their laurels and return from whence they came, and Sheriff Peppin without the confidence of the people or even himself retreats to Fort Stanton at which place he is under the care and protection of the soldiers--

I find that Gov. Axtel[l] acted in the interests of the Murphy, Dolan, & Riley party and was strictly partisan and that the charge is sustained--

Charge Sixth--I report that this charge has been sustained as already set forth--

Charge Seventh--I report that this charge has been sustained as appears by facts set forth under Charge Fifth--

Charge Eighth--Under this charge is the appointment of Col. Chaves and Peppin. It was rumored that Col. Chaves had falsified the election returns and as a reward he was nominated and appointed Territorial District Attorney. There is however no evidence of this fact and I accordingly report that as to this part of the charge the same is not sustained. But that as to Peppin the charge is sustained.

The Governor replies that he appointed Peppin under recommendation of W. L. Rynerson (testimony p. 6). Rynerson is undoubtedly a good lawyer and a gentleman but he is never the less a strong partisan and his record in the Lincoln County troubles show that he has used his office for oppressive purposes. The Governor must have known this, therefore with knowledge of Peppin's character he acted again strictly partisan and appointed an improper man --

Charge Ninth--I find has been sustained as appears from facts set forth herein—

Charge Tenth—As to this charge there are no substantial facts to show that he is a Mormon. I therefore report that the source is not sustainable—

Charge Eleventh--On considering this charge we must go back in the unwritten history of New Mexico to the time when Colfax County by the arbitrary and unlawful acts of certain officials, became too hot for them, and they had to leave the County for the County's good. The plan was devised and carried out to join Colfax County to Taos County for judicial purposes and a bill was rushed through the Legislature and signed at once accomplishing this design. Immediately the people at Cimarron telegraphed Gov. Axtell "<u>Requesting him to withhold his signature until a delegation from Colfax could wait upon him</u>." The reply came back "<u>Bill signed, S. B. Axtell</u>." If there was trouble in Colfax County which could not be quieted then there was a justification in having this bill--it would have then been an excellent measure. But the facts show that when this bill was passed the troubles in Colfax Co. had been quieted and stopped and that there was more lawlessness in other parts of the Territory than in Colfax (testimony pp. 22, 23-48).

<u>No benefit resulted from the charge</u>—but on the contrary it was a gross injury and injustice to the people of Colfax County—The two counties are separated by a range of high mountains, the lowest pass 9000 feet in altitude, which when the court is in session are difficult and dangerous to cross. It required a journey over these mountains of 54 miles to reach court. The juries were entirely taken from Taos County, manipulated by Pedro Sanches, a ringite, and prejudiced by outside influence.

There never could be a fair trial in criminal proceedings and all most all civil business was suspended (testimony pp. 24-27). It was a great expense to Colfax Co. for witnesses and fee--

CAUSE AND EFFECT

It is surprising that opposition to the arbitrary Governor arose and with opposition came vindictiveness and revenge on the part of the opposed—

The Governor was visited at Santa Fe said he was heartily in favor of the bill and spoke with extreme bitterness about the people of Colfax County--and refused to go to Colfax Co. and investigate the facts for himself saying "<u>He was fully advised about matters in that County and didn't need further information</u>" (testimony p. 25).

After this at a public meeting at Cimarron an invitation in courteous language was addressed to the Governor inviting him to visit Colfax County and make a thorough investigation for himself. This invitation was signed by ten or twelve prominent citizens. To this the Governor makes no reply or acknowledgement (p. 28).

--At this stage Ben Stevens, territorial District Attorney and appointee of the Governor appears.

--He circulates the report that he is going to try and have the Governor visit Colfax, leaves Cimarron, goes to Fort Union, and returns in a few days with a company of soldiers (colored) and exhibits a telegram from the Governor which reads as follows: "<u>Do not let it be known that I will be in Cimarron on Saturday's coach. Body guard all right</u>" and said it was proof that the Governor was coming to visit the County and would expect to meet those who had signed the invitation and that they must be on hand on the arrival of the coach to meet him. He requested that the matter be kept quiet as the Governor did not want a crowd but only wanted to meet those who had invited him (pp. 29-30-31).

The facts subsequently show that the Governor did not intend to visit Colfax Co. and that the action of Stevens was in furtherance of a plot as will appear by the following letter--

Dear Ben--the second telegram delivered to you at Fort Union directed to Cimarron was intended to leak but the operator here says he cannot raise the Cimarron office. If I was expected, our friends would probably be on hand, as the guard is only a Government escort. I do not think your definite business is expected. Wade informed Hatch that he has been ready all the time to assist you, but could not find that you wanted to do it. Hatch says their opinion is that you weakened and do not want to arrest the man. Have your men placed to arrest him and to kill all the men who resist you or stand with those who do resist you. Our man signed the invitation with others who were at the meeting, for me to visit Colfax-- Porter, Morley, Springer, *et.al*. Now, if they expect me Saturday, they will be on hand. Send me letters by messenger, and do not hesitate at extreme measures. Your honor is at stake now, and a failure is fatal. If others resist or attempt murder, bring them also. Hatch is excited and wishes to put all the blame on the civil officers. I am more anxious on your account than for any other reason. I clearly see that we have no friends in Colfax, and I have suspected all along that some of our pretended friends here were traitors.

Yours, & c., S. B. Axtell

--Was there ever a cooler devised plot with a Governor as sponsor? The Governor admits the letter in toto [*Sic*] (pp. 56-9) "<u>That it sounds like me</u>" (p. 9) and then subsequently attempts to explain away part of its terrible features (p. 9).

He makes no attempt as to the telegram. Nor why he wished it to "<u>leak</u>". But by a down right falsehood he attempts to assemble certain persons who are obnoxious to him so that in the event, of the resistance to be arrested, of a person by the name of Allison [infamous Clay Allison] as excuse would be offered "<u>to kill all the men who resist or stand with those who resist you.</u>"

He does not explain this -- he cannot--

Stevens and the soldiers were sent by Governor Axtell ostensibly to arrest a person by the name of Allison-- but reading the foregoing telegram and letter I do not believe that it was the real object, for Allison was afterwards arrested and at once set at liberty (p. 35) and Governor Axtell subsequently made an appointment and traveled with said Allison in a friendly way in the stage coach (p. 36)--

Any man capable of framing and trying to enforce such a letter of instructions as the one set forth in this report is not fit to be entrusted with any power whatever-- I therefore report that this charge has been sustained--

Charge Twelfth--On February 1876, a bill was passed through the Legislature providing that the Courts should be removed from Cimarron, Colfax County to Taos, Taos County and that after two terms the Governor might at his option restore the Courts to Colfax County. For the reasons set forth under Charge Eleventh, I find that under this charge is sustained—

In conclusion, I respectfully submit that whether through ignorance or corrupt motive the actions of said Axtel[l] has been to keep many parts of the Territory of New Mexico in a state of turmoil and confusion, when intelligent and non-partisan action on his part might have avoided much of the difficulty, and that the removal of Governor Axtell viewed with the evidence and his reply received before my first report, was an absolute necessity, and it becomes still more evident that such was the right course on receiving his subsequent replies—

It is seldom that history states more corruption, fraud,

mismanagement, plots, and murders than New Mexico has been the theatre under the administration of Governor Axtel[l]—

I transmit herewith the testimony herein—

All of which is respectfully submitted--

Dated Washington, Oct. 3, 1878

[signed] Frank Warner Angel

Special Agent

Department Interior

Index page

Angel, F. W.	1
Axtell, S. B.	41
Amt. of crime in Territory & C	48
Beardsley, E. I.	87
Charges filed March 29, 1877	94
Gilliland, F. G	61
Hunt, E.	93
Interrogatories to Gov. Axtell	2
Leverson, M. R.	64
Lee, W. D.	84
Norton, J. B.	90
Proclamation removing Wilson	8
Proclamation removing Copeland	59
Shields, D. P.	110
Springer, F.	78--49--12
South, W. L.	86
Taylor, J. L.	91

Whigham, H. 74

So reads Angel's charges and conclusions against the Territorial Governor, S. B. Axtell. The Governor was removed and replaced by Lew Wallace who wrote at least a part of his famous book, *Ben Hur* while occupying the Governor's Palace in Santa Fe.

Samuel B. Axtell: Governor of the Territory of New Mexico until replaced by Lew Wallace after Angel's report was reviewed in Washington. (Courtesy of the Museum of NM)

APPENDIX C—THE CHARGES AGAINST F. C. GODFROY

The following are Frank Warner Angel's conclusions concerning the charges against F. C. Godfroy, Indian Agent for the Mescalero Apaches. Also included is the index of the letters, statements, and affidavits collected during the investigation:

In the matter of the examination of the charges against

C. F. Godfroy [Frederick C.]

```
Indian Agent Mescalero Apaches
               N. M.
```

To the Honorable C. Schurz, Secretary of the Interior

--I have the honor to submit my report in relation to the charges against C.F. [F. C.] Godfory Indian Agent Mescalero Apaches New Mexico---

CAUSE AND EFFECT

--Mr Godfroy stands charged as follows---

First

--Of allowing or loaning large quantities of Government property to private individuals--

Second

--Of fraudulently representing that there were more Indians on the reservation than there actually exist and of claiming to issue rations to this fraudulent number -- appropriating to his own use the difference between the amount actually issued to bona fide Indians and their alleged number--

--<u>As to these charges</u>, the evidence is very conflicting. Mr. Godfroy admits that during the time he has been Indian agent he has loaned to various parties government goods to the amount of at least ten thousand (10,000) pounds but claims that the same has invariably been returned in kind and quantity--

--<u>There</u> are many suspicious circumstances connected with these transactions which throw great doubt on their honesty, and whether various persons have not perjured them selves in order either to clear Mr. Godfory , on paper, or to convict him of these charges—

I. When I first visited the agency the accusation that Mr. Godfroy had sold or loaned any government property was absolutely denied both by him and his family. Afterwards, they admitted that goods have been loaned--

II. The only record of these transactions were memoranda kept on slips of paper and these slips destroyed, although both Mr. Godfroy and the principal parties to whom it is alleged he loaned the property kept regular books--

III. The testimony of various witnesses who testified as to the return of the goods impressed me that they were not telling me what they actually knew but what someone had posted them to say.--

IV. The subsequent discovery by me of from ten (10) to thirteen thousand (13,000) pounds of government property at Las Lunas, N. M. which is claimed to have been taken from this Indian agency, and the evidence is circumstantially strong as to this fact--

V. The number of Indians by actual count (under unfavorable circumstances) being only three hundred and seventy three (373) whereas it is claimed many hundreds [of] rations are issued to Indians on issue days--

CAUSE AND EFFECT

<u>VI</u>.--The relationship of Mr. Godfory with Murphy, Dolan, and Riley and--

<u>VII</u>.--The lack of credibility and responsibility of some of the witnesses both for and against Mr. Godfroy--

--Yet with all these suspicions I am strongly impressed to the belief that Mr. Godfroy has not loaned the government property, but has by fraudulent numbers in the Indians, appropriated and sold vast quantities of government property to his own private gain and advantage--

<u>Certainly</u> by his own admission he stands convicted of using government property improperly--

--<u>He</u> cannot claim that these goods were disposed without his knowledge by his clerk Bernstein.

-- Such large quantities could not be removed without his knowledge or some member of his family--

--The evidence as far as numbers of witnesses are concerned is in his favor-- so far as weight and credibility it is about equally divided--

--I have carefully gone over the evidence in order if possible to give him the benefit of the doubt. An educated and cultured gentleman surrounded by a loving and refined family, it is hard to believe that he has been so guilty, but the more I read the testimony and the circumstances connected with it the stronger is my convictions that he is a guilty man--

--It however can be said in his behalf, in extenuation or lightening his punishment, that he is the best Indian agent that the government has so far as control and care of the Indians are concerned.--

Under his care depredations and lawless acts of the Indians have ceased. Under the able tuition of his daughter many children and not a few grown people belonging to the tribe are educated and taught to love and fear God and their proficiency as witnessed by me was truly remarkable--

--The Indians are taught and encouraged in the various industries are well cared for--love and respect their agent and are easily controlled and influenced by him. He has not starved them-- He supplies them liberally and the farmers in the county can thank this agent for the preservation of their lives and property by his control over these Indians

--<u>I would therefore most respectfully report</u> in consideration of the premises that the charitable benefit of the doubt be given him and rather than do him an irreparable wrong under the conflicting evidence that he be requested and allowed sufficient time to tender his resignation and that in default thereof he be removed--

I transmit herewith the testimony taken herein—

--All of which is respectfully submitted

--Dated Washington October 2, 1878

(signed)   Frank Warner Angel

Special Agent

Department of Interior

Index

Page

Angel, F. W.	95
Ayers, J.	83
Blazer, Jos. H.	19
Bernstein, M. J	19-53

Grady E. McCright

Bartlett, C. H.   103

Boyle, A.   134

Burt, J. G.   139

Baca, S   142

Carroll, H.   27

Carter, G   79

Dolan, J. J.   111-39

Dudley, N. A. M.-106

Evans, J. J   114

Ervan, R. H.   140

Farmer, Jas. H.   7

Godfroy, F. C. 128-99

Gallegos, P   31

Mathews, J. B   125

Peppin, G. W   7-51

Riley, J. H. -   131

Romero, E   87

Stanley, S   1

Trujullo, S   118

Washington, Geo.   15

Watkins, E. C   94

Widermann, R. A.
[Widenmann]   75

As the result of this report and Angel's recommendation, Godfroy was asked for his resignation which he promptly delivered. The Agent, thereby, avoided prosecution for the charges levied against him.

Frederick C. Godfroy: He served as Indian Agent for the Mescalero Apache Reservation from July, 1776 until September, 1878 when allowed to resign as a result of Angel's report. (Courtesy of the Old Lincoln county Memorial Commission)

APPENDIX D—CHARGES AGAINST DR. B. M. THOMAS

The following are Frank Warner Angel's conclusions concerning the charges against Dr. B. M. Thomas, Indian Agent for the Pueblo Indians of New Mexico. Also included is the index of letters, statements, and affidavits collected during the interviews.

Investigation:

In the matter of the examination of charges against

Dr. B. M. Thomas

U. S. Indian Agent Pueblo Indian of New Mexico

The said Thomas is charged as follows:

First

--That he has used and appropriated Government property to his personal and private use-- Testimony pages 1-5-6-7-10-18-20

Second

--That he has procured and entered fraudulent vouchers--Testimony pages 2-14-22-

Third

--That he does not take proper care or protect government

property-- Testimony pages 14-21-25

Fourth

--That while occupying his own house he has led the Government to believe that he did not own it, and has put in fraudulent vouchers for rent-- Testimony pages 7-14-16-17

I Dr. Thomas meets charges 1, 2, and 3 by a full and explicit denial and explanation, and although there are two witnesses who swear to these charges, I am constrained to believe in the light of the high certificates of character given by leading men of Santa Fe, by persons who would not certify to his honesty and integrity unless they knew it to be true, that he is entitled to every presumption and the benefit of every doubt, and that these witnesses against him distorted and warped the facts for private spite--

II. I therefore most respectfully report that charges 1, 2, and 3 are not sustained--

III. As to charge 4-- I am not disposed to look so lightly on –

He must have known that he was doing wrong and as a Christian and a man he has been guilty of deceit--

--He admits this charge. He could not deny it, but says "I knew that if I furnished a better agency than could be had any other way I was entitled to reasonable rent for it. I made the mistake of getting vouchers in another name. I did it because I understood that to be the custom in such cases and to prevent caviling & C"(Testimony page 25).

--Custom never makes wrong right nor does it justify deceit because someone else has done wrong it is no excuse.

--His action is censurable more than censurable [SIC]. It is not the amount involved, it is the principal at stake--

--I believe that his conscience has punished him sufficiently. I believe that it will not occur again. I know that he has rendered valuable services to the government in assisting in the removal of the Ute and Apache Indians from Cimarron. I believe that the certificates of character hereto attached are true. I know that they are made by reliable and honest men--

IV. <u>I therefore report that this</u> false step-- this charge should be condoned and that Dr. Thomas be retained in his office—

--I herewith transmit the Testimony in relation to these charges--

--All of which is respectfully submitted

-- Dated Washington October 1, 1878

(signed) Frank Warner Angel

Special Agent

Department Interior

Index

Page

Atkinson, H. M. (letter)---------------34

Breeden, M. A. (letter)---------------30

Conway, John W. (affidavit)-------------1

Carter, Chas. (affidavit)----------------------------------10

Fiske, E. A. (letter)---------------------------28

Garica, M. (affidavit)-------------6

Griffin, W. W. (letter)-----------------8

Irvine, Alex G. (affidavit)-----------16

Menuiel, John (statement)----------26

Presbytery, Santa Fe (letter)---------32

Roberts, Jas. H. (statement)----------26

Grady E. McCright

Shields, J. M. Rev. (statement)------26

Smith, G. A. (letter)----------------------37

Thomas, B. M. (affidavit)-----------18

This investigation of Dr. Thomas resulted in his being chastised for claiming rent on the home which he owned; however, he was allowed to remain in the Department of the Interior's Indian Service. As recommended by Angel, all other charges were dismissed.

APPENDIX E—WALLACE'S NOTEBOOK

When Angel met with Governor Lew Wallace before the latter took control of the New Mexico Territorial government, he took the governor's address book and supplied his impressions of the people he had met during his recent trip to the Territory. Angel also listed his thoughts about newspapers in the area.

This address book is now in the hands of the Indiana Historical Society in Indianapolis. The fact that Wallace kept the book instead of discarding it soon after his term as New Mexico governor indicates that he had reason to believe that the document someday would have historical significance. It is presented here with almost all the original spellings but with some additional formatting made for clarity.

Alberquerque *Review*—Independent

News & Press-- Cimmarron Ind[ependent]--not a very high tone paper. It is against the gov.[Axtell]

Las Vegas *Gazette*--Republican--favors the ring

Santa Fe *New Mexican*-- Ring paper Republican

The Sentinel--Santa Fe Independent

Santa Fe *News*—Democratic

The Independent--Mesilla--Independent

Mesilla News--Ring Paper

Andrews, Enos--Santa Fe--reliable

Ayers, John--Honest--liquor his worst enemy--

Axtel, S. B.--[Gov. Axtell]--Santa Fe--Conceited—egotistical. easily flattered --Tool unwittingly of the ring--goes off "half cocked"

Arney, W. F. M.--Santa Fe-- The great American lier [liar]--look out for him. No power or influence. Runs the [Governor's] Palace for Axtel [Axtell]

Atkinson, H. M.--Santa Fe Surveyor Gen.--Honest and very reliable. Only official who courted investigation.

Boyle, Andrew--at present in Mesilla—Outlaw—murderer

Blazer, Jos. H.--Lincoln Co.—Reliable--knows a great deal--will not tell what he knows

Bartlett, Chas. H.--Lincoln Co.—Honest

Barrier, Adolph P.—Las Vegas – Dept. Sheriff—favors McSween party—has acted for the right so far

Beardsley, Ezra I.—Cimmarron—Not reliable—Ex Post master--master A/c [accounts??] not correct Since has been made all O. K.

Breeden, M. A.--Santa Fe --post master, weak ring man--can be led with a string

Breeden, Col.--Santa Fe--I do not think he is reliable

Bristol, W.--Mesilla--Ass. Justice--Honest & reliable out side of Lincoln troubles

Beckwiths—Pecos--look out for the old man. The boys are honest & reliable out side of Lincoln troubles

Bull--Mesilla--reliable--square man

Berillia--Sheriff at Mesilla--not reliable, ring tool

Carroll, Henry Capt.--Hatch man--Fort Stanton--Reliable outside of Hatch matters.

Coghlan, Pat--Honest great friend of Murphy party--Godfroy & that crowd--resides at Tulerosa

Cline--Lincoln reliable--I do not think he is mixed up in the Lincoln troubles

Copeland, John M.--Sheriff removed by Gov.—Lincoln--McSween party--I think reliable

Chaves, A.—-Albuquerque--Territorial Dist. Atty—Strong ring man--Has a reputation of altering election returns 1875

Crouch, Jno A.—Mesilla—U.S. Clerk=Editor—Mesilla *Independent*—Trickist. Not reliable in every respect

Conway, Thos.--Santa Fe—lawyer--some ability, I think reliable

Coe boys—Lincoln--I think are reliable especially Frank

Chison, John S. [Chisum]—Pecos--backbone of McSween party—sharp--be careful with him

D'Sena, Jose D.--Santa Fe politician--considerable influence not entirely reliable

Davis, Geo.--Lincoln outlaw--murderer

Dorsey, S. W.--near Cimarron—Senator--be careful with him

Dolan, J. J—Lincoln--Leader in Lincoln Co. trouble--Murphy party--brave, sharp--determined fellow--Badly mixed up with the ring & c.

Dudley, N. A. M.--Fort Stanton Post Commander--However mortal enemy of Hatch--talks too much--rely on him rather than Hatch

Dowlin, Will--Post trader Fort Stanton--Honest, reliable --is Co. Commissioner

Delgado, F.--Santa Fe--I think reliable--great church man

Evans Jessie--Lincoln Co.—outlaw--murderer

Ellis—Lincoln--There are two of these persons--McSween men but I think they are good citizens and reliable

Elkins, S. B.—"Silver Tongued" further comment unnecessary

Elkins, John—brother of S. B.—Honest but dependent upon brother—Strong ring man

Eley, Rev. [Ealy]--at Las Vegas—weak--not reliable--McSween man

Ellison, Sam--Santa Fe—weak--tool of Catron

Fields, Westley--Lincoln Co.--I think is reliable

Farmer, Jos. H.--Lincoln Co.--honest

Fiske E.--A Santa Fe--lawyer—Shrewd--honest reliable--can be of great service to you--He controls the U. S. Marshall. Has been of a great service to me--Well posted as to the people and the frauds in the territory

Fisher--Santa Fe--of Fisher & Lucas--reliable

Gallegos, Panteleon--not reliable--in employ of Dolan--a tool

Godfroy, C. F. [F. C.]--Indian agent near Ft. Stanton--Badly mixed up

Gonsoles, F. [Gonzales]--Probate Judge Lincoln--reliable

Grace, Fred--Santa Fe--Politician

Griffin, W. W.--Santa Fe--Reliable & honest in 1st Nat. Bank & is influenced by Elkins

Howe, Albert H.--Lincoln Co.--I think reliable

Hurley, John—Lincoln--easily influenced--Murphy party

Hill, John—Albuquerque--Under ring influence

Hubbel, Judge--Las Vegas--I think reliable--likes his "toddey" I think reliable

Hatch, E.—Santa Fe Dist. Commander—Dudley's mortal enemy—Rumors of his fraud and corruption—To be handled with gloves

Hockraddle, Jerrie—Murphy man but honest & I think reliable

Jones—Mesilla--Catron's tool--not reliable

Kriling, Chas.—Pecos--honest but not reliable

Liverson, M. R. [Leverson]--Now on his ranch, Larkspur, Colo.--knows 6 times more than he can prove & 6 times more than any one else--He can be of service to you USE HIM--Don't commit yourself--STRONG McSween man "THE GREAT AMERICAN LETTER, NEWSPAPER, & C WRITER."

Lee, Wm. D.—Cimarron--reliable but weak under influence of Springer

Loud, Lieut.--Santa Fe. Officious--Works for the ring--not reliable

Longwell, Dr.--Santa Fe. Good Dr.--but mixed up in Colfax trouble. Axtel [Axtell] man, ring man--do not rely on him

Lucas--Santa Fe--of Fisher & Lucas--very reliable a square man

Laugon, "Judge"--Santa Fe—reliable--but I think a democrat

Mathews, J. B.--Dept. Sheriff Lincoln. Partisan Murphy party

Montano, Jose—Lincoln—I think reliable

Matterson, M—Socorro—Minister. Has done good work at Socorro & I think reliable

McPherson, Mrs, M. E.—Washington, D. C. Not reliable—Is interested or mixed up in Colfax troubles

McDaniels, Jim—Lincoln--desperado

Murphy, L. G.--Santa Fe--Mixed up in Lincoln Co.--Now a drunkard--no reliability--He belives himself a martyr and McSween the devil--Handle him with gloves

McMullen, Wm.--Santa Fe--Not reliable

McSween, Mrs.--Lincoln now at las Vegas--Sharp woman now that her husband is dead a tiger USE HER HOWEVER ("MOLASSES CATCHES MORE FLIES THAN VINEGAR")

McCandless, Chas.--Santa Fe. Sup. Judge--VERY reliable--good man to work with

Michaels, Dr.—Cimarron--Sharp fellow--Axtell man

Newcomb, John—Lincoln—Honest--McSween party--I think reliable

Patron, J. B.—Lincoln--Has considerable influence with Mexicans--not entirely reliable

Perry, S. R.—Pecos--I think reliable-- but of no standing

Probst--Santa Fe—Honest—reliable--but shallow

Parington, G. A. [Purington]--Fort Stanton Captain--Honest but is a Hatch man

Pippin, G. W.—Present Sheriff—Lincoln Co.—weak—Murphy man—Partisan not reliable

Romero, T.—Delegate influenced by Elkins

Tomero, R.—*La Cueva*—Smart young man. I think reliable--

"Roxey"—Lincoln--outlaw

Riley, J. H.--Las Cruces--Sharp, cunning fellow also leader of Murphy party Lincoln--Very dissipated-- not reliable--interested with Catron in Gov. contracts

Ritch, W. G.--Santa Fe--Sec. Territory--Axtell man--otherwise reliable

Rynerson, W. L.--Territorial Dist. Atty Mesilla—strong Partisan Axtell man--Murphy man--has used his office oppressively--not reliable.

Stanley, Steph.--Lincoln D. B.—dishonest--drunkard

Sherman, John Jr.--U. S. Marshall Santa Fe (bro. of Secy) means to tell all he knows—reliable--but not much backbone unless "braced up" Use him through Fiske.

Springer, F.—Cimarron—Reliable—educated--runs Cimarron--Very hostile to Gov. Axtell

Shields, D. P.--Las Vegas--Brother-in-law McSween--I believe reliable

Smith, G. A.--Santa Fe--U. S. Collector--old foggy used by Catron--makes good returns to Government--not reliable

Spiegelberg Bros.--Santa Fe--Not reliable--use them agst [against] Z. Staab Bros. & vice versa

Stabb, Z & Bro—Santa Fe—Axes to grind—not reliable—use them agst [against] Spiegelberg Gro & vice versa

Smith, G. G. –Santa Fe—Pastor Presp Church—I do not believe he is realiable

Strachan, W. J.--Santa Fe--a democrat but I think reliable--Catron's enemy

Thompkins, R. H.--Santa Fe—honest & I think reliable--old age against him

Thornton, W. T.--Santa Fe--Catron's partner

Thayer, Chas.--Santa Fe Gambler--honest & I think reliable

CAUSE AND EFFECT

Upson, M. A.—Roswell--Smart but dishonest--not reliable

Wilson, Andrew--Lincoln Co.--Reliable

Wakefield, E. H.--Las Cruces--has mail contract from there to Ft. Stanton--easily influenced--Murphy party--I think he means to be honest

Widenman, R. A. [Widenmann]--Now at Mesilla--Great friend of McSween--given to boasting, veracity doubtful when he speaks of himself--well connected in the east & well educated

Whigham, Henry—Cimarron--Editor Cimarron *News & Press*--Not very reliable unless backed by Frank Springer McSween man

Waldo, H.--Santa Fe--Present Atty Gen—Honest--good lawyer and reliable but great friend of Axtel [Axtell]

Wilson, J. B.—Lincoln Justice of Peace--"Old Fox" and very WEAK easily influenced. On the fence

West, Jas.—Lincoln--honest & I believe reliable

Watts, J. H.--Santa Fe--I think he is reliable

Waltz, E. A.—Lincoln--a tool of Catron--a boy--not reliable

Angel's insight is remarkable. He met most of these persons and took testimony from most, but his exposure to them was limited to a day or so at best. Much of his impressions must have been gleaned from depositions of others and in conversations from locals; nevertheless, his knowledge of the characters involved with the Territory is impressive.

One glaring omission in the Wallace notebook is the exclusion of any personal entry for Thomas B. Catron, United States Attorney of the Territory at the time. Catron was very involved in the Colfax County cover up and eventually resigned due to Angel's findings. Catron is mentioned a number of times as having influence over others men described in the content but there is no entry giving Angel's feelings about the U. S. Attorney. Was this lack of comment an oversight or did Angel merely discuss Catron's involvement with Wallace and because it was so strong, he , perhaps, decided not to include any observations in writing? We will never know for sure.

CHRONOLOGY

1824

____: John S. Chisum born

1827

April 10: Lewis Wallace born, Lexington, Massachusetts

1831

____: Lawrence Gustave Murphy born in Ireland

1833

____: Andrew L. "Buckshot" Roberts born

1840

October 6: Thomas Benton Catron born near Lexington, Missouri

1845

_____: Frank Warner Angel born in New York City.

1852

June 24: Robert A. Windenmann born in Ann Arbor, Michigan

1853

March 6: John Henry Tunstall born in London, England.

1861

____: L. G. Murphy joins New Mexico Volunteers at Fort Union as 1st Lieutenant

1864

July 2: Frank Angel receives Bachelor of Arts degree from Free Academy of the City of New York.

November: L. G. Murphy promoted to Major

1866

____: Thomas Catron arrives in the Territory

____: Emil Fritz and Dolan muster our of Army at Fort Stanton

1867

____John S. Chisum arrives in the Territory

1869

____: L. G. Murphy evicted from Fort Stanton and establishes a small mercantile in Lincoln in the house destined to become McSween's residence. He continues as unauthorized post trader and postmaster at Fort Stanton

____: Frank Angel admitted to the New York Bar.

1873

____Alexander McSween is a Justice of the Peace in Eureka, Kansas and marries Sue E. Homer of Atchison, Kansas

September 2: Murphy finally physically evicted from Fort Stanton

Fall: Murphy starts building "the Big House" mercantile in Lincoln. The firm finally opens in June, 1874

1875

March: The McSween couple arrive in Lincoln

CAUSE AND EFFECT

1876

July 1: Frederick Godfroy assumes the Indian Agent post at the Mescalero Apache reservation

November 6: John Tunstall arrives in Lincoln

1877

Mid-February: Widenmann reaches Lincoln

March 14: Murphy retires from the "Big House"; Dolan now in charge

May: Murphy makes out his will with Dolan as sole beneficiary

August: Tunstall opens mercantile store and bank with Chisum and McSween.

1878

February 6: Dolan threatens to kill Tunstall at Shedd's Ranch.

February 18: (about 5:30 p.m.): John H. Tunstall killed.

February 22: Tunstall buried.

April 1 (morning): Sheriff Brady and deputy ambushed.

May (early): Special Agent Frank W. Angel arrives in the territory.

May (mid): Angel arrives in Lincoln.

May-June: Angel takes testimony and investigates incident.

July 14-19: Five-day battle in Lincoln. McSween and others killed.

July (late): Angel probes Colfax County problems.

August 11: Angel questions Governor Axtell about his involvement in Colfax County problems.

August 14: Angel leaves for New York.

August 24: Angel arrives home and begins to compile his report.

September (early): Angel meets with President Hayes in Washington.

September (mid): Lew Wallace replaces Axtell as New Mexico Territorial Governor.

September (late): Mescalero Indian Agent Frederick Godfroy resigns.

October 10: Thomas Catron resigns.

October 30: L. G. Murphy dies of natural causes.

1879

February 18 (night): Peace of some sort is agreed to and then shortly after, Mrs. McSween's lawyer, Huston I. Chapman killed on Lincoln street.

1881

July 14: William Bonney, alias Billy the Kid, killed by Sheriff Pat Garrett in Fort Sumner.

.

1882

August 1: Axtell appointed New Mexico Chief Justice.

1884

December 20: John S. Chisum dies.

1886

January: Tunstall family receives final word that the United States Government will not admit any liability for Tunstall's death.

January 1: Frank Angel appointed Fire Commissioner of Jersey City.

1891

August 6: Axtell dies.

1898

February 26: James J. Dolan dies

.

1903

_____: Angel becomes Commissioner of Appeals in Jersey City.

1906

January 1: Angel resigns from Board of Appeals because of bad health.

March 15 (5:30 a.m.): Frank Angel dies at home.

1912

_____: Thomas Catron elected to the United States Senate.

1921

May 21: Thomas Catron dies.

Grady E. McCright

FOOTNOTES

1. Frederick W. Nolan, *The Life and Death of John Henry Tunstall*, p.274.
2. Alexander A. McSween and his wife, Susan, moved to New Mexico in the spring of 1875 from Kansas where he had suffered from asthma. He began his law practice immediately, prospered and gained quite a reputation. He was Tunstall's attorney and partner in the bank but he had no money invested in the store.
3. The men who located Tunstall's body packed it on a horse to Newcomb's ranch, then transferred it to a wagon. This took all day so the body did not arrive in Lincoln until after nightfall. Angel said Newcomb was "Honest-McSween party-I think reliable." Angel's short descriptions quoted in the first sixteen or so footnotes are from "Frank Warner Angel's Notes on New Mexico Territory, 1878."
4. Dr. D. M. Appel was the post surgeon at Fort Stanton and his examination noted no bruises on Tunstall's head or body even though Dr. Ealy said Tunstall's head was badly mutilated and R. Widenmann testified that the skull had been smashed. Dr. Taylor F. Ealy, a physician and minister, had only arrived in Lincoln with his family on February 19. Angel classed him as "weak-not reliable-McSween man."
5. Robert A. Widenmann and Tunstall had met in Santa Fe and although he was not in Tunstall's hire, he lived at the

ranch and dabbled in this and that. Few people liked Widenmann because of his parasitic ways. However, his letters to Secretary of Interior Carl Schurz carried weight because Schurz and Widenmann's fathers were friends. Angel said he was "great friend of McSween--given to boasting-veracity doubtful when he speaks of himself--well connected in the east & well educated."

6. Angel Report, Department of Justice, File #44-4-8-3, National Archives, Washington, D.C. This letter is dated March 9, 1878. In all quoted material from Judge Angel's Report the author attempted to retain Angel's formatting. Sometimes this was difficult due to the printed page versus Angel's hand written report.
7. Montague R. Leverson, from Great Britian, was staying at Chisum's while he scouted for a suitable place to establish a colony of settlers. He was from Colorado and took no real part in the conflict except for his poison pen to Federal and British officials after Tunstall's death.
8. Leverson became known by Angel as "The great American letter and newspaper writer." because of his poison pen with which he dispatched numerous epistles to Washington and to the local newspapers. Letter to President Hayes cited in Frederick W. Nolan, *The Life and Death of John Henry Tunstall*, 295-296.
9. Leverson to Schurz, April 1, 1878, Angel Report, Op. Cit.
10. Leverson to Hayes, April 1, 1878, Angel Report, Op. Cit. This letter is written on paper bearing Juan B. Patron's letterhead.
11. Leverson To Hayes, April 2, 1878, Angel Report, Op. Cit. This letter is 10 legal-size pages in length.
12. Thornton to Evarts, March 27, 1878, Angel Report, Op. Cit.
13. Evarts to Devens, April 3, 1878, Angel Report, Op. Cit.
14. Phillips to Evarts, April 9, 1878, Angel Report, Op.Cit.
15. John Simpson Chisum came to New Mexico from Texas and claimed almost 200 miles of Pecos River grassland. He was a business partner of Tunstall and McSween yet he was not an active participant in the war. Angel said of him,

"Backbone of the McSween party-sharp-be careful with him."
16. Lawrence G. Murphy was an Irishman whose career in the military terminated at Fort Stanton where he became the post trader. Angel said of him, "Mixed up in Lincoln County-now a drunkard-no reliability-he believes himself a martyr and McSween the devil-Handle him with gloves." His first partner, was Emil Fritz but he was long since dead. Murphy then took up with J. J. Dolan. Murphy died on October 30, 1878, in Santa Fe, of natural causes. Because of his poor health, Murphy actually played only a small part in the war--his influence played a much larger role. Angel said of Dolan, "Leader in Lincoln Co. trouble-Murphy partner-brave-sharp-determined fellow-badly mixed up with [Santa Fe] ring." John H. Riley became a partner in the firm in 1877. Angel said of him "Sharp cunning fellow also leader of Murphy party-very dispatched-not reliable-interested with Catron in Gov. contracts."
17. Lee Scott Theisen, "Frank Warner Angel's Notes on New Mexico Territory", *Arizona and the West*, 334. Original notebook is in the possession of the Indiana Historical Society.
18. Maurice G. Fulton, *History of the Lincoln County War*, p. 236.
19. *Ibid.*, 237.
20. Nolan, *Op. Cit.*, 339.
21. Letter to authors from Barbara Dunlap, Archivist, The City College of New York City. A Chronology of the Lincoln County War, p. 25.
22. Fulton, *Op. Cit.*, 238.
23. Nolan, *Op. Cit*, p.344.
24. *Ibid,*. pp. 340-341
25. *Ibid,,* p339.
26. Robert N. Mullin, *Op. Cit*, p 25
27. Cleaveland, "The Great New Mexico Cover Up," p. 5.
28. .Theisen, *Op. Cit.*, 335.
29. *Ibid.*, 336.
30. Fulton, *Op. Cit.*, 249.

31. The board talked to the men in the Wortley Hotel, which included James Dolan and Jessie Evans. They claimed they had seen the entire incident and that McSween's forces had fired the shot. Interview with Herman Weisner, 1979.
32. Fulton, *Op. Cit.*, 259-260. Mullin, Op. Cit., 26. Mullin says it was 10 a.m.
33. It is obvious that McSween was not a military strategist. It is strange that so many seasoned men would follow his directions for so long in view of the mistakes he made. Billy the Kid finally stepped forward and salvaged some lives, but, even then, it was too little--too late.
34. Grady E. McCright, "Lincoln County Hysteria," *Rio Grande History*, Number 9, 19-21.
35. Leon C. Metz, *Pat Garrett, The Story of a Western Lawman*, 51. Metz tells a different story. He says that Jessie Evans and James Dolan shot Chapman, then poured whisky on the body and set the clothes on fire during the evening of the 18th. Troops from Fort Stanton retrieved the body at about 11:30 on the night of the 19th, more than 24 hours later, according to Fulton, *Op. Cit.*, 37.
36. Metz, *Op. Cit.*, 117.
37. Mullin, *Op. Cit.*, 35. Patron's killer was a Texas cowboy named Mitch Maney.
38. Angel Report, *Op. Cit.*
39. The affidavits of: Alexander A. McSween, Juan B. Patron, Florencio Gonzales, Robert A. Widenmann, Jose Montano, George Vansickle, and Godfrey Gauss.
40. Juan B. Patron affidavit.
41. Florencio Gonzales affidavit.
42. The affidavits of: McSween, Widenmann, Patron, and Albert H. Howe.
43. McSween affidavit.
44. The affidavits of: McSween, A. P. Barrier, J. J. Dolan. Dolan, of course, states that he never dropped his carbine on Tunstall and did not threaten him. Among other exhibits attached to McSween's affidavit is a check, numbered 300, drawn on the 1st National Bank of Santa Fe, dated July 31, 1877. It is made payable to William Brady, Sheriff and Ex-officio Collector, Lincoln

45. McSween and Widenmann affidavits.
46. James J. Longwell affidavit.
47. McSween affidavit.
48. J. B. Mathews affidavit. It provides a list of employees at Tunstall's ranch:
    a. Robert Widenmann
    b. William Bonney
    c. Dick Brewer
    d. William McClosky
    e. Dutch Martin
    f. _____ McCormick
    g. Henry Brown
    h. Godfrey Gauss
    i. Fred Waite
    j. John Middleton
49. Widenmann places the number of cattle at Tunstall's at between 400 and 500.
50. Those named by Mathews as in his second posse in addition to himself were:
    a. John Hurley*
    b. Manuel Segovia*
    c. George Hindman*
    d. A. L. (Buckshot) Roberts
    e. Pantaleon Gallegos*
    f. James J. Dolan**
    g. A. H. Mills
    h. J. W. Ollinger*
    i. Thomas Moore
    j. R. W. Beckwith*
    k. Ramon Montoya*
    l. Felipe Mes
    m. E. H. Wakefield
    n. Pablo Pino y Pino,
    o. Baker*and Long* Although earlier in his affidavit he admits they were riding in his posse. Some affidavits also say that George Davis rode with the Evans-Hill foursome.
    *These Men rode with Morton after Tunstall's horses.
    **From some accounts, J. J. Dolan did not ride with the

posse but came to Tunstall's ranch during the night after Tunstall had been killed.
51. John Patton affidavit, as told to him by H. H. Howe. Howe stated that George Kitt related to him that, "Tunstall was murdered in cold blood by Morton and Hill."
52. While numerous affidavits in the report support Angel's statement that Tunstall's death was not the result of resisting a lawful process, the page cited (228) in his cover letter does not. This is a page from the affidavit of Sam Perry, a posse member. It reads, "I believe that under the circumstances above set forth that Tunstall met his death while resisting a legal process."
53. Theisen, *Op. Cit.*, 333-370.
54. Report from Angel to the Department of the Interior.
55. *Ibid.*
56. Catron to Devens, October 10, 1878, File #44-4-8-3.
57. *Op. Cit.* Nolan, *Tunstall*, p. 436.

BIBLIOGRAPHY

BOOKS AND ARTICLES

Cleveland, Norman. *The Great Santa Fe Cover Up*, privately published, 1982.

Cleveland, Norman. *An Introduction to the Colfax County War*, 1875-1878, privately printed, 1975.

Cleveland, Norman. "The Great New Mexico Cover-up", *Rio Grande History*, Number 5, New Mexico State University, Summer 1975.

Ball, Eve, *Ma'am Jones of the Pecos*, The University of Arizona Press, Tucson, 1973.

Fulton, Maurice Garland. *History of the Lincoln County War*, Edited by Robert N. Mullin, University of Arizona Press, Tucson, 1969.

Klasner, Lily, *My Girlhood Among Outlaws*, Edited by Eve Ball, University of Arizona Press, Tucson, 1972.

McCright, Grady E. and James H. Powell, "Disorder in Lincoln County," *Rio Grande History*, Number 12, New Mexico State University, 1981.

McCright, Grady and James H. Powell, *Jessie Evans, Lincoln County Badman,* Creative Publishing, College Station, 1983

McCright, Grady E. "Lincoln County Hysteria," *Rio Grande History*, Number 9, New Mexico State University, Spring 1978 (Lincoln County Issue).

Keleher, William A, *Violence in Lincoln County, 1869-1881*, University of New Mexico Press, Albuquerque, Second edition, 1957.

Metz, Leon C. *Pat Garrett, The Story of a Western Lawman*, Norman, University of Oklahoma Press, Norman, 1974.

Mullin, Robert N. *A Chronology of the Lincoln County War*, Santa Fe, Press of the Territorian, 1966.

Nolan, Frederick W. *The Life and Death of John Henry Tunstall*, University of New Mexico Press, Albuquerque, 1965.

Nolan, Frederick W. "A Sidelight to the Tunstall Murder," *New Mexico Historical Review*, July 1956.

Sonnichsen, C. L. *Tularosa, Last of the Frontier West*, The Devin-Adair Co, Old Greenwich, Conn., 1960.

Theisen, Lee Scott. "Frank Warner Angel's Notes on the New Mexico Territory," *Arizona and the West*, Volume 18, Number 4, Winter 1976.

Utley, Robert M. *High Noon in Lincoln*, University of New Mexico Press, Albuquerque, 1987.

HISTORICAL RECORDS

Angel Report, Department of Justice, File #44-4-8-3, National Archives, Washington, D.C.

"The Examination of Charges Against C. F. Godfroy, Indian Agent, Mescalero, N.M.", National Archives, Record Group 75, Bureau of Indian Affairs, New Mexico Letters Received in 1878.

National Archives, Bureau of Indian Affairs, Group 75, Letters Received from New Mexico Territory, 1878-1879.

New Mexico Territorial Papers, U.S. Department of Interior, Letters Received April 1852-May 29, 1907.

Philip Rasch Papers, Old Lincoln County Memorial Commission, Lincoln, New Mexico.

LETTERS RECEIVED

Thomas J. Candiloro, City of Jersey City, N.J., Division of Fire, September 8, 1978.

Joan F. Doherty, Jersey City Public Library, April 17, 1978.

Barbara Dunlap, City College of New York, March 7, 1978.

Sheldon Greenberg, First Assistant District Attorney, Brooklyn, N.Y., February 28, 1978.

Daniel J. Jacobs, New York Bar Association, February, 1978.

Raymond P. Maloney, Acting Fire Director, Jersey City, N.J., April 13, 1978.

INTERVIEWS

Molly Madden, Old Lincoln County Memorial Commission, Lincoln, N.M., December 1975.

Robert N. Mullin, South Laguna, California, September 1975 and October 22, 1975 (telephone).

Donald Mosholder, National Archives, Washington, D.C., 1976 (telephone).

Lee Scott Theisen, National Archives, Washington, D.C., 1976 (telephone).

Herman Weisner, Organ, New Mexico, May 1979.

ABOUT THE AUTHOR

Grady E. McCright: As did many of the Lincoln County gunfighters, the author arrived in New Mexico from Texas in 1966. He was immediately enamored with both the country and the history. In 1983, he and co-author James H. Powell published *Jessie Evans, Lincoln County Badman*, Creative Publishing Company, College Station, Texas.

Over the years, McCright has written and published 6 additional books of western fiction and western-historical fiction under both his own name and the pen name of Ira Compton. All of these fiction books are available in paper and Kindle format from Amazon. After a more than 32 year career with the National Aeronautics and Space Administration (NASA), McCright and his wife Marie retired to Cloudcroft, New Mexico in 1998.

Other Books by Grady E. McCright

Jessie Evans, Lincoln County Bad Man, by Grady E. McCright and James H. Powell, Creative Publishing Company, College Station, Texas, 1983

*A Stranger Rides In, by Ira Compton (Pen Name), Western Fiction, 1997

*Paco, The Apache Tracker, by Ira Compton (Pen Name), Historical Fiction, 1997

*Widow's Plight, by Ira Compton (Pen Name), Western Fiction, 2000.

*The Salt War, Unrest in El Paso, by Ira Compton (Pen Name), Historical Fiction, 2000.

*Sign of Passage, Punitive Expedition into Mexico after Pancho Villa in 1916, by Grady E. McCright, Historical Fiction, 2008

*Massai: The Last Apache Outlaw, by Grady E. McCright, Historical Fiction, 2008

*The Whirlwind, John Lapham Bullis and his Seminole-Negro Scouts, 2012.

NOTE: All are available from Amazon.com.

*Kindle format as well as paper

Made in the USA
Lexington, KY
27 March 2015